"That love is inexhaustible, you will be there"

forever

_____

_____

_____

_____

_____

THIS BOOK Belongs to

_____

_____

Visit Our Author Page At
amazon.com

All rights reserved. No part of this book may be used or reproduced in any manner whatsoever without written permission except in the case of brief quotations embodied in critical articles and interviews.

© by **BLACK ROSE PRESS HOUSE**

SKYSCRAPERS COLORING BOOK

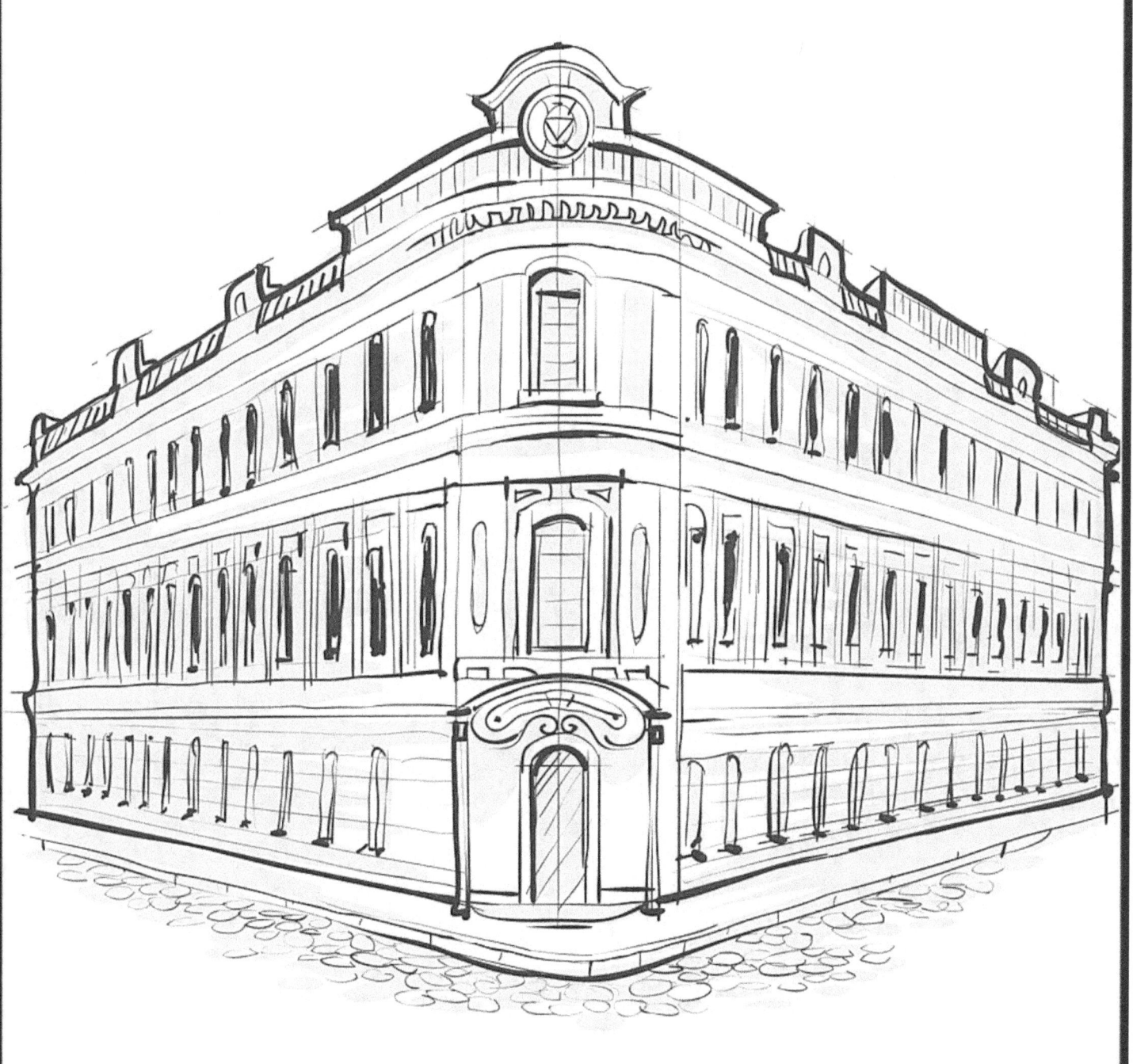

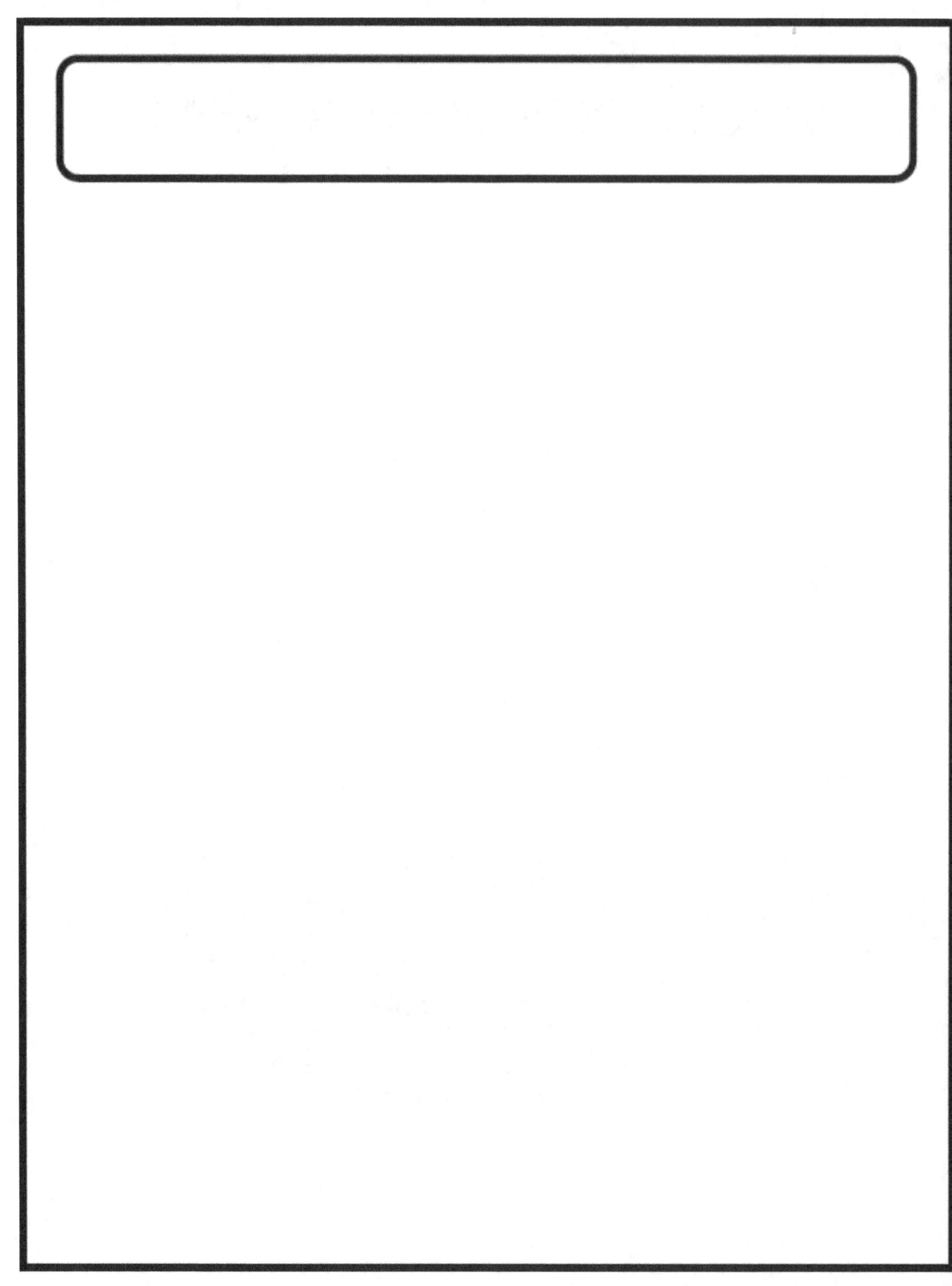

SKYSCRAPERS COLORING BOOK

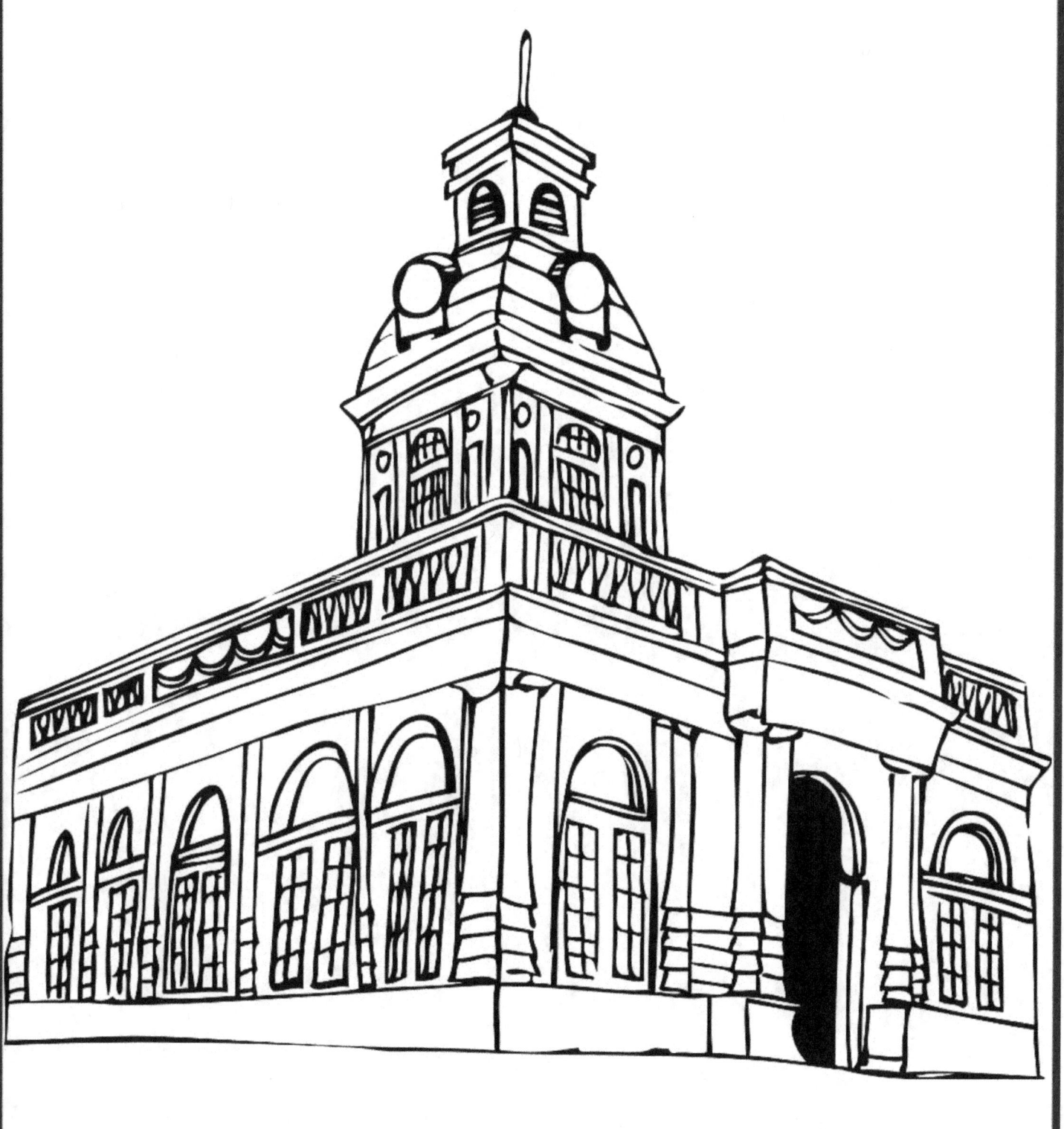

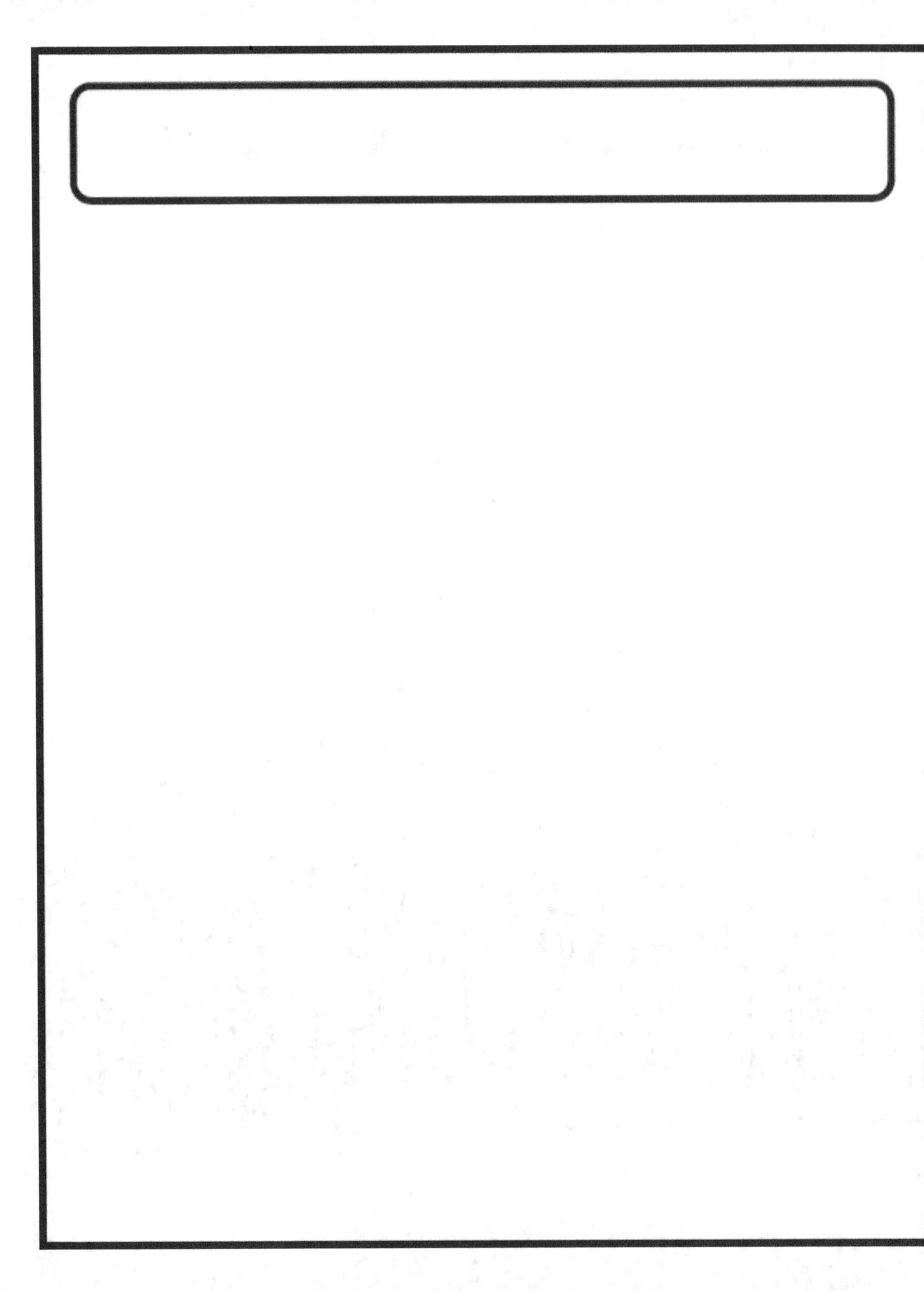

SKYSCRAPERS COLORING BOOK

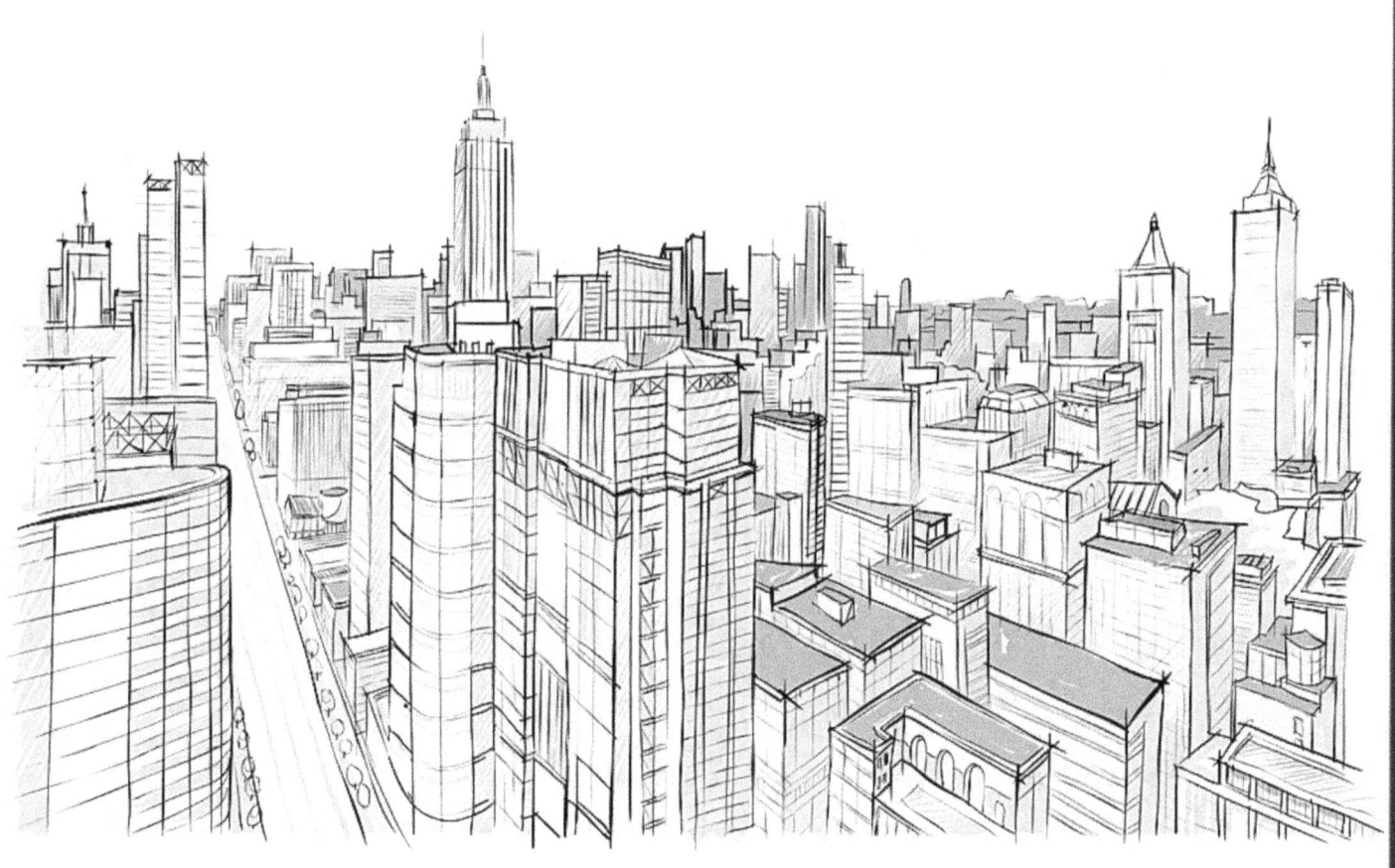

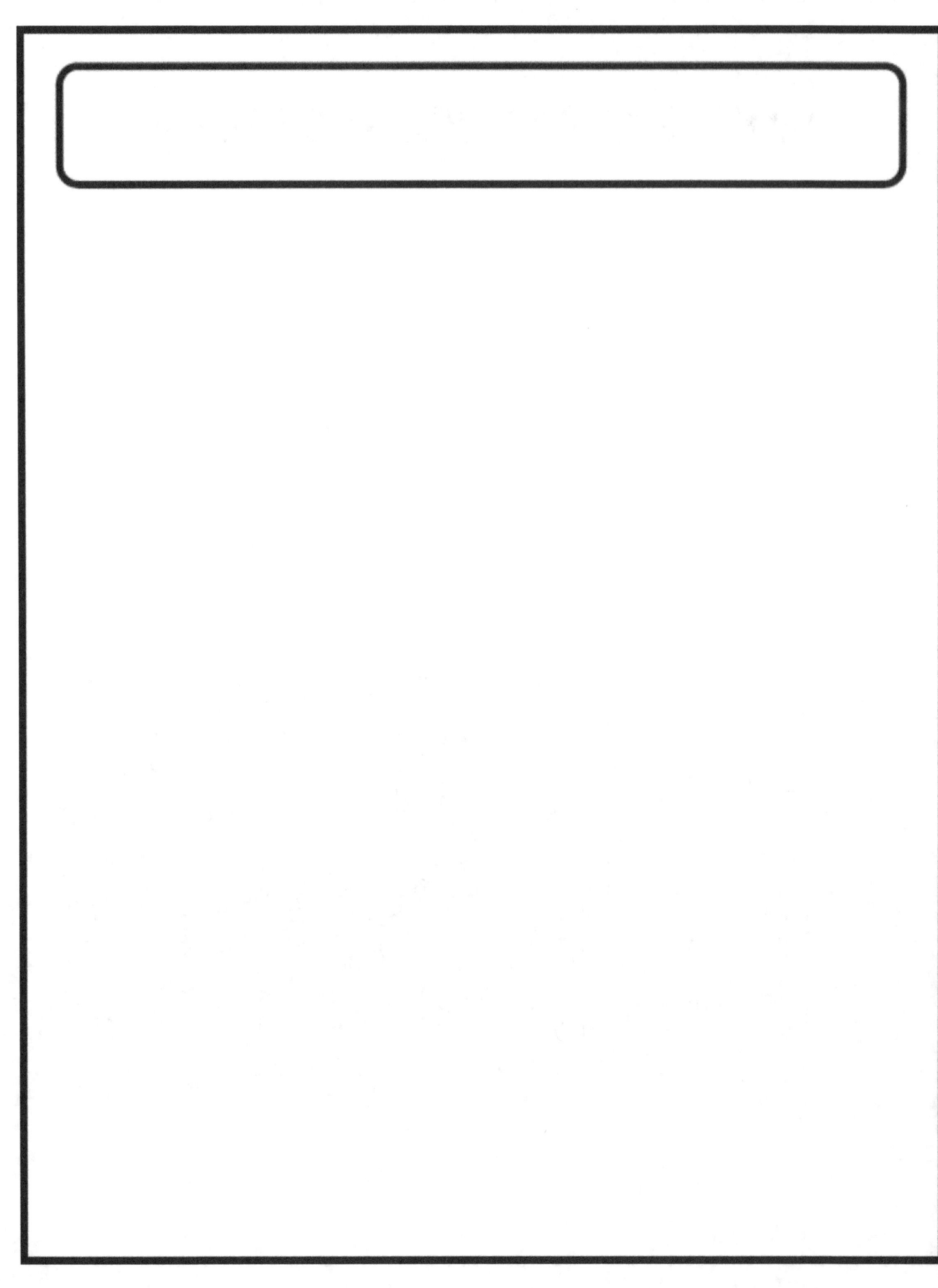

SKYSCRAPERS COLORING BOOK

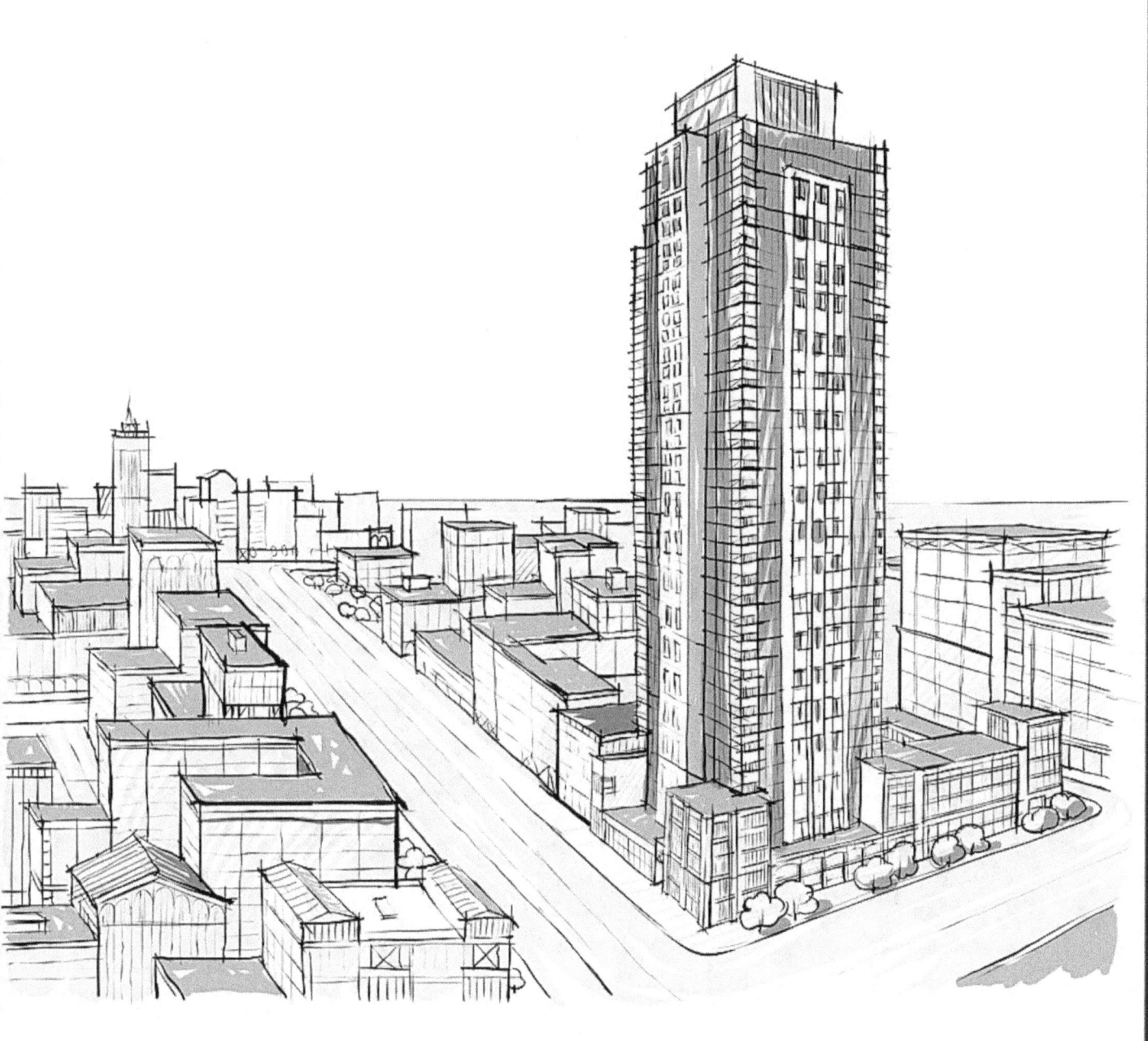

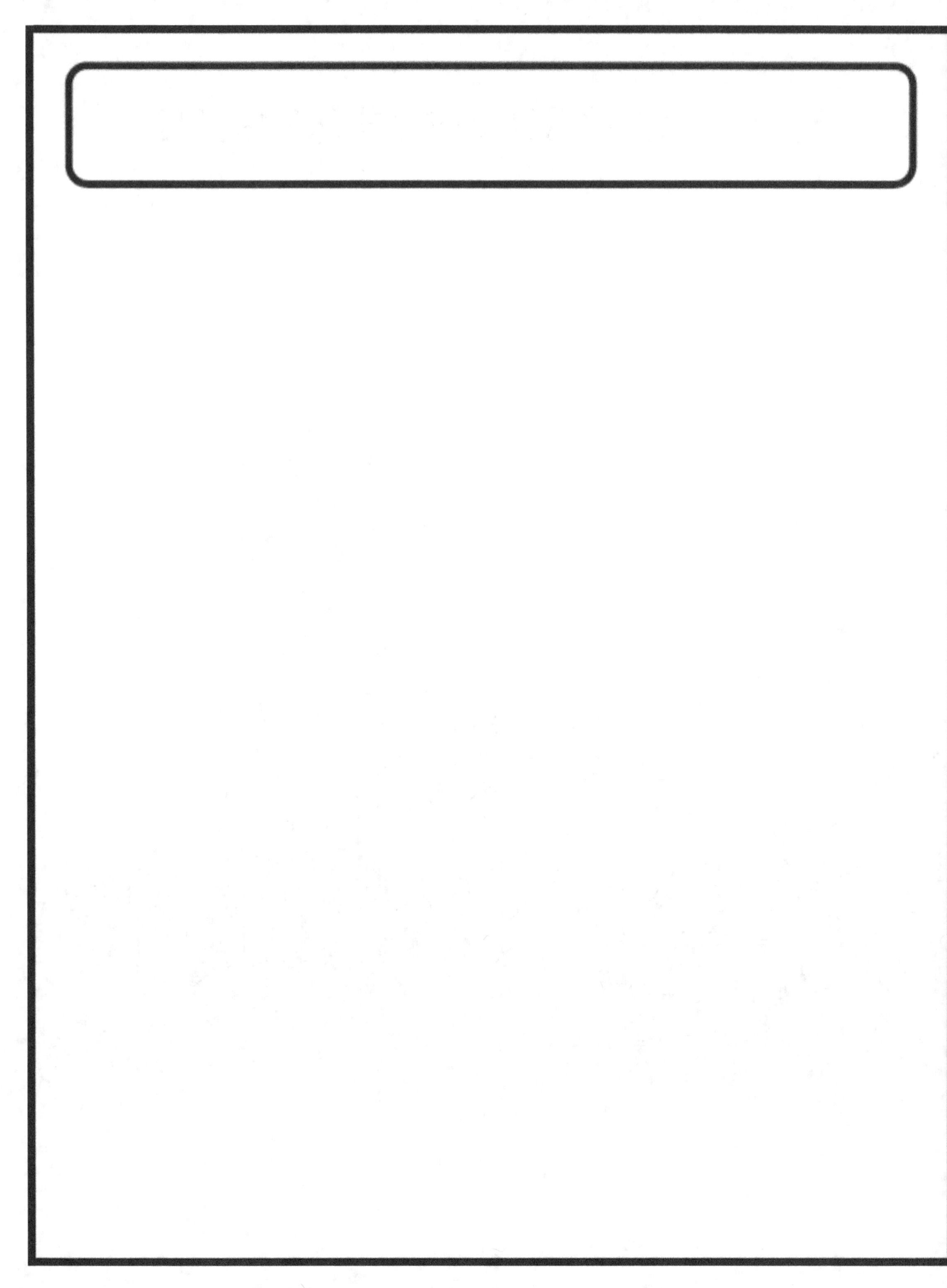

SKYSCRAPERS COLORING BOOK

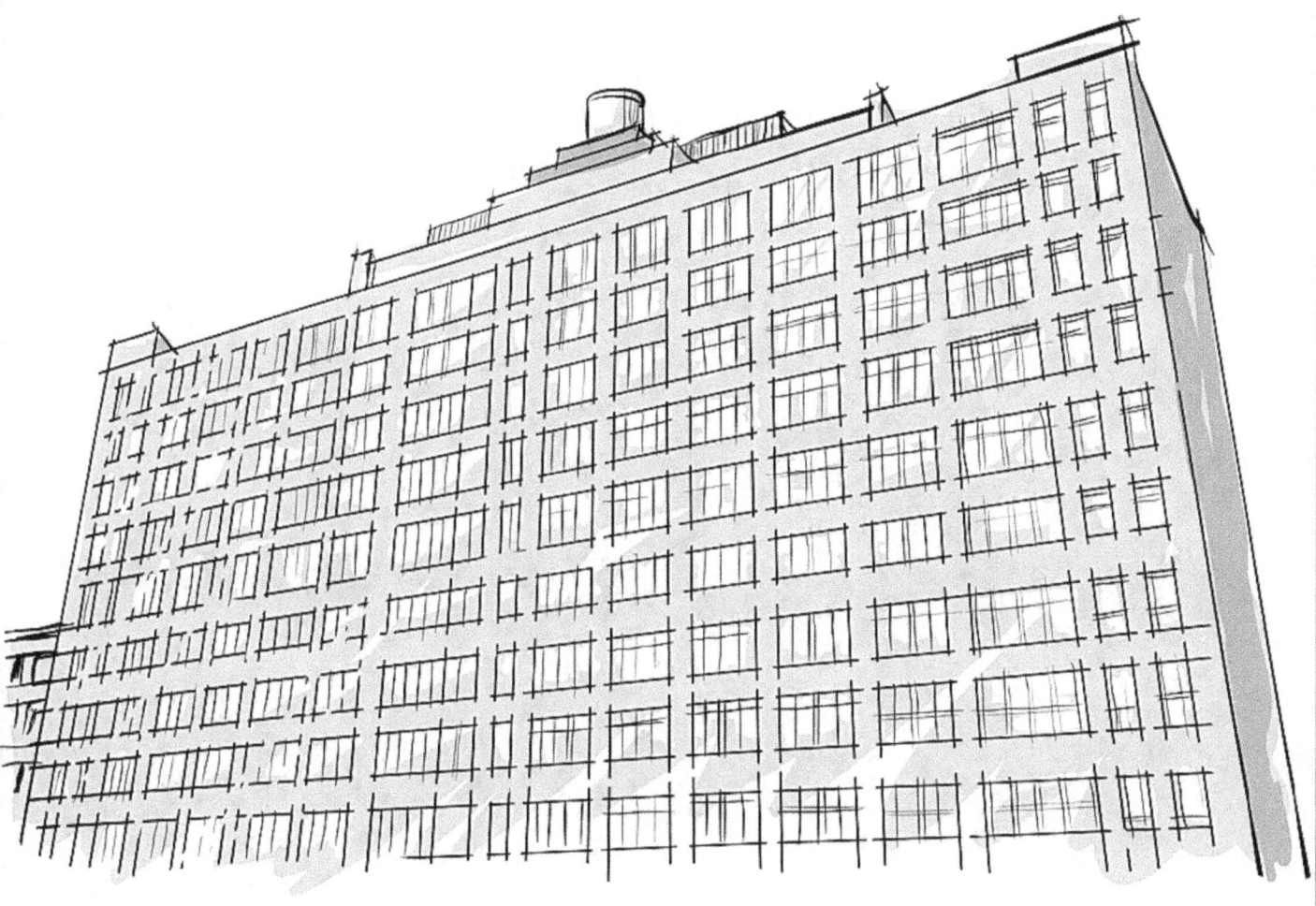

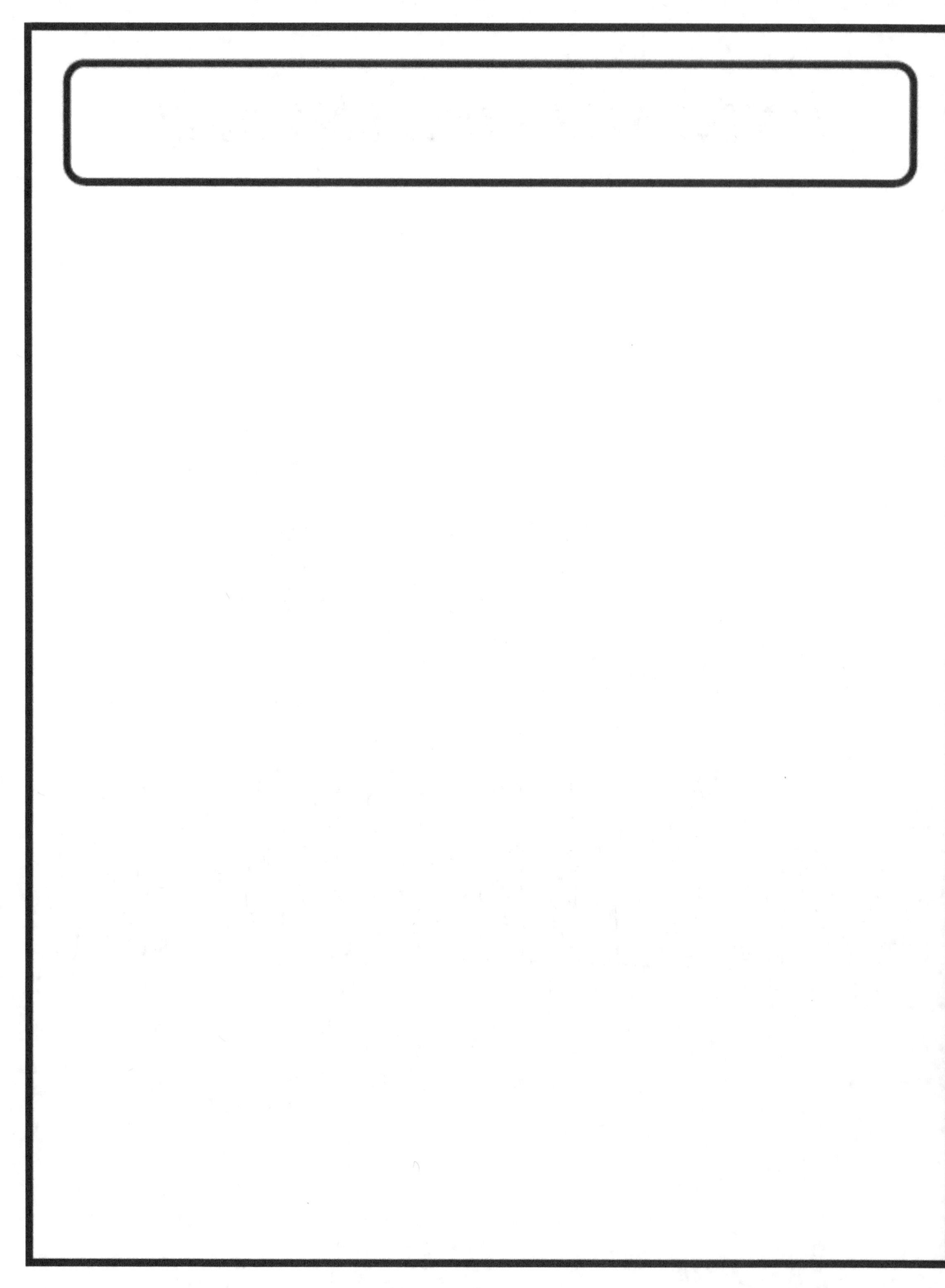

SKYSCRAPERS COLORING BOOK

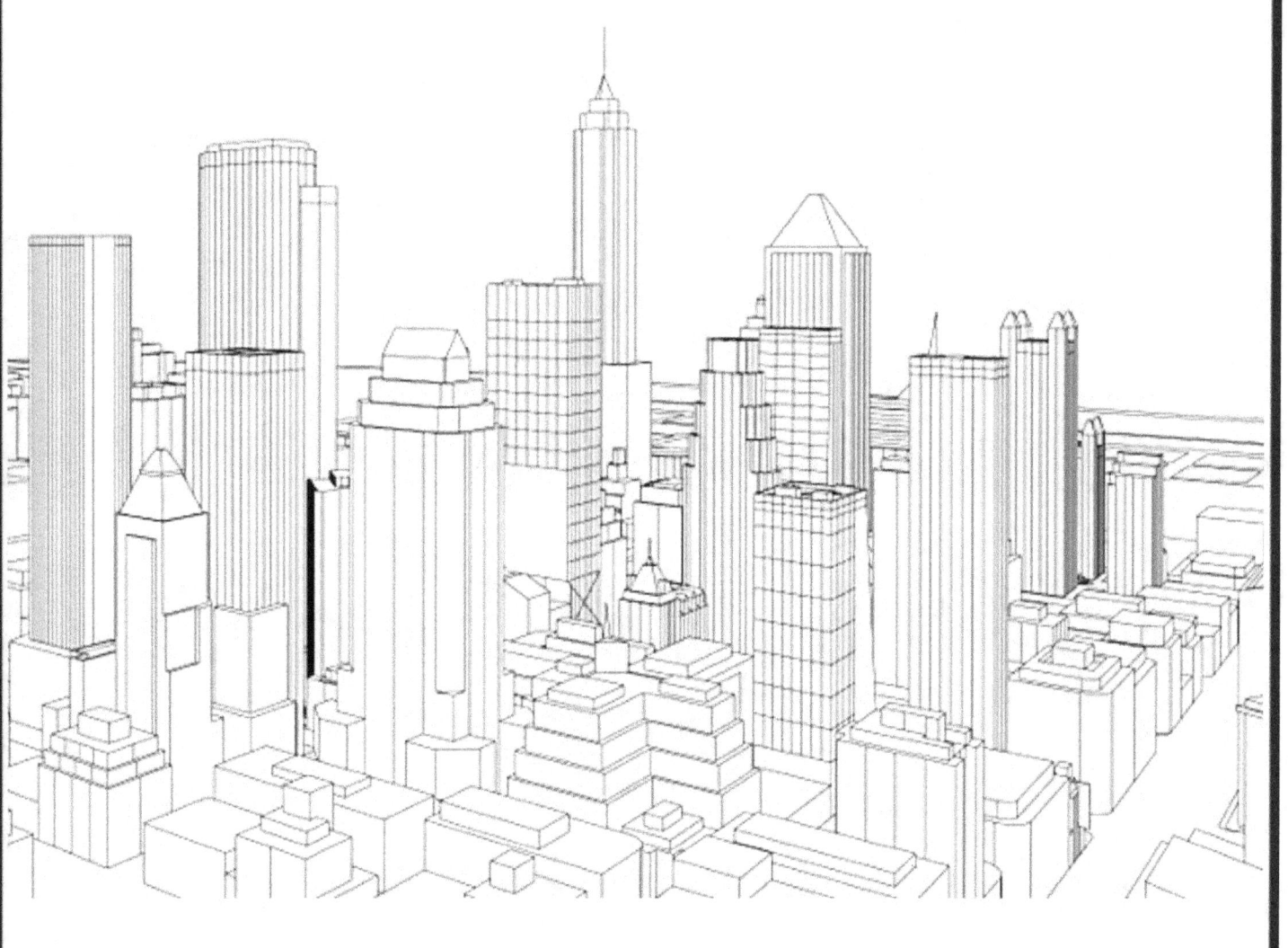

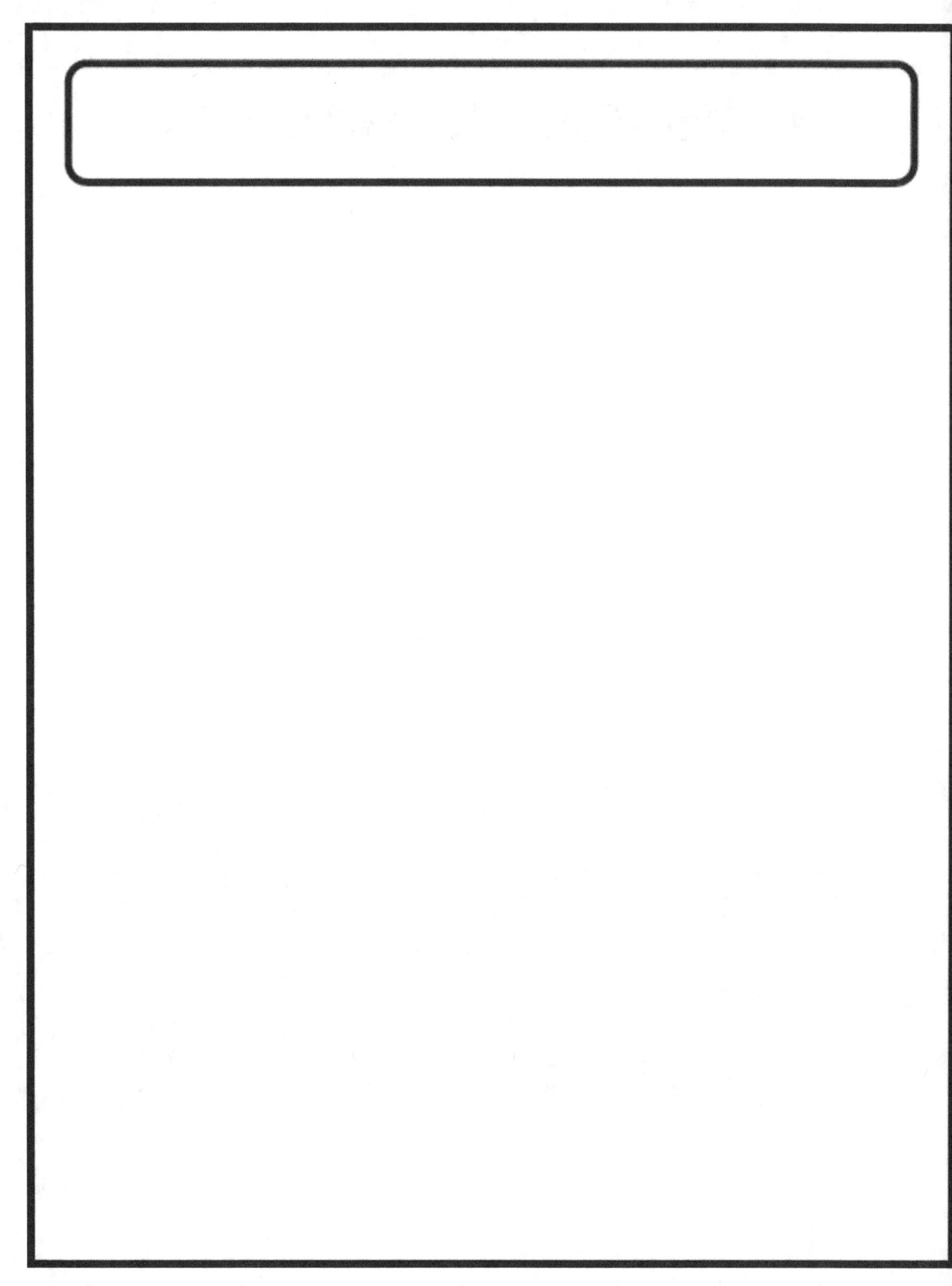

SKYSCRAPERS COLORING BOOK

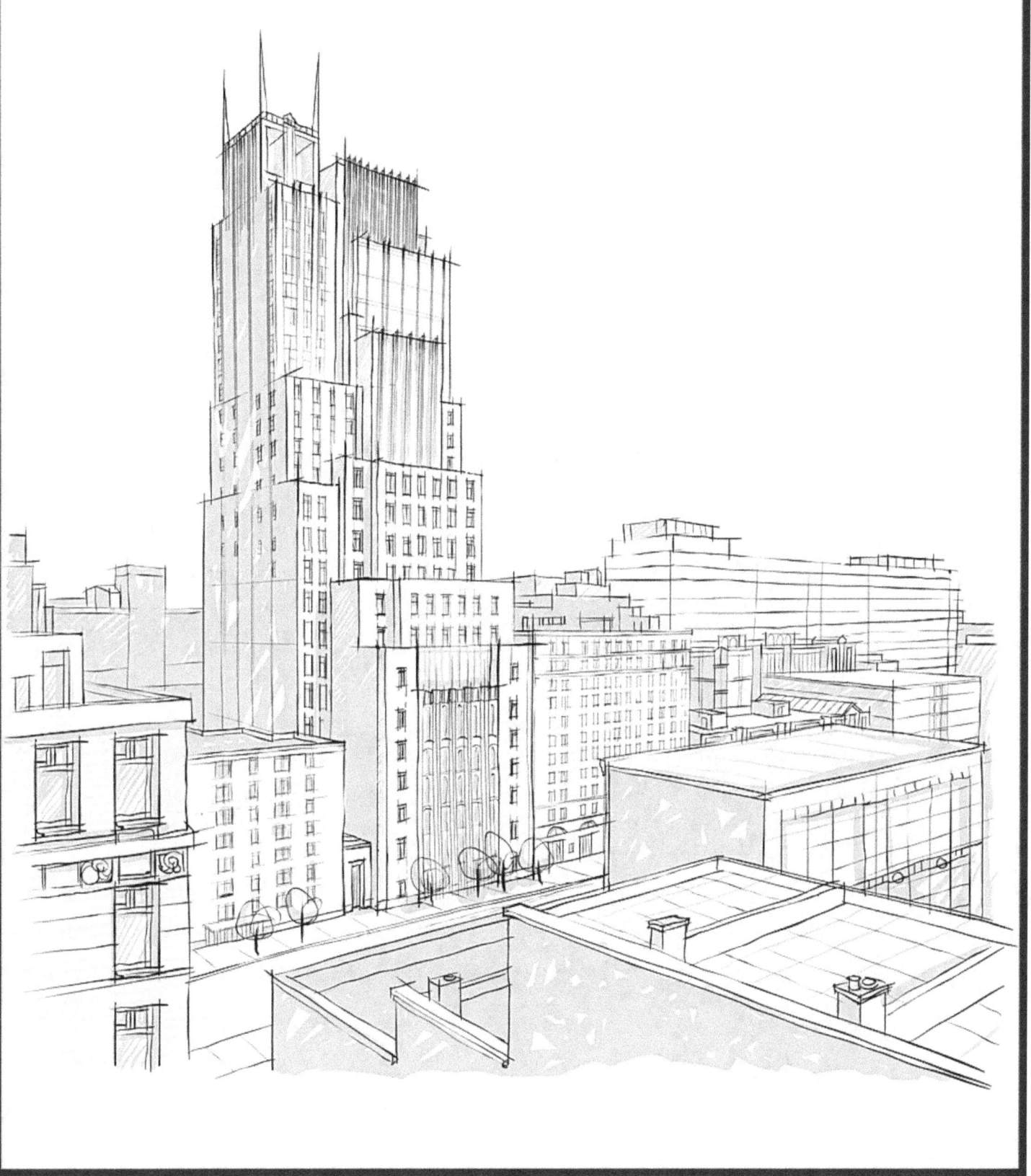

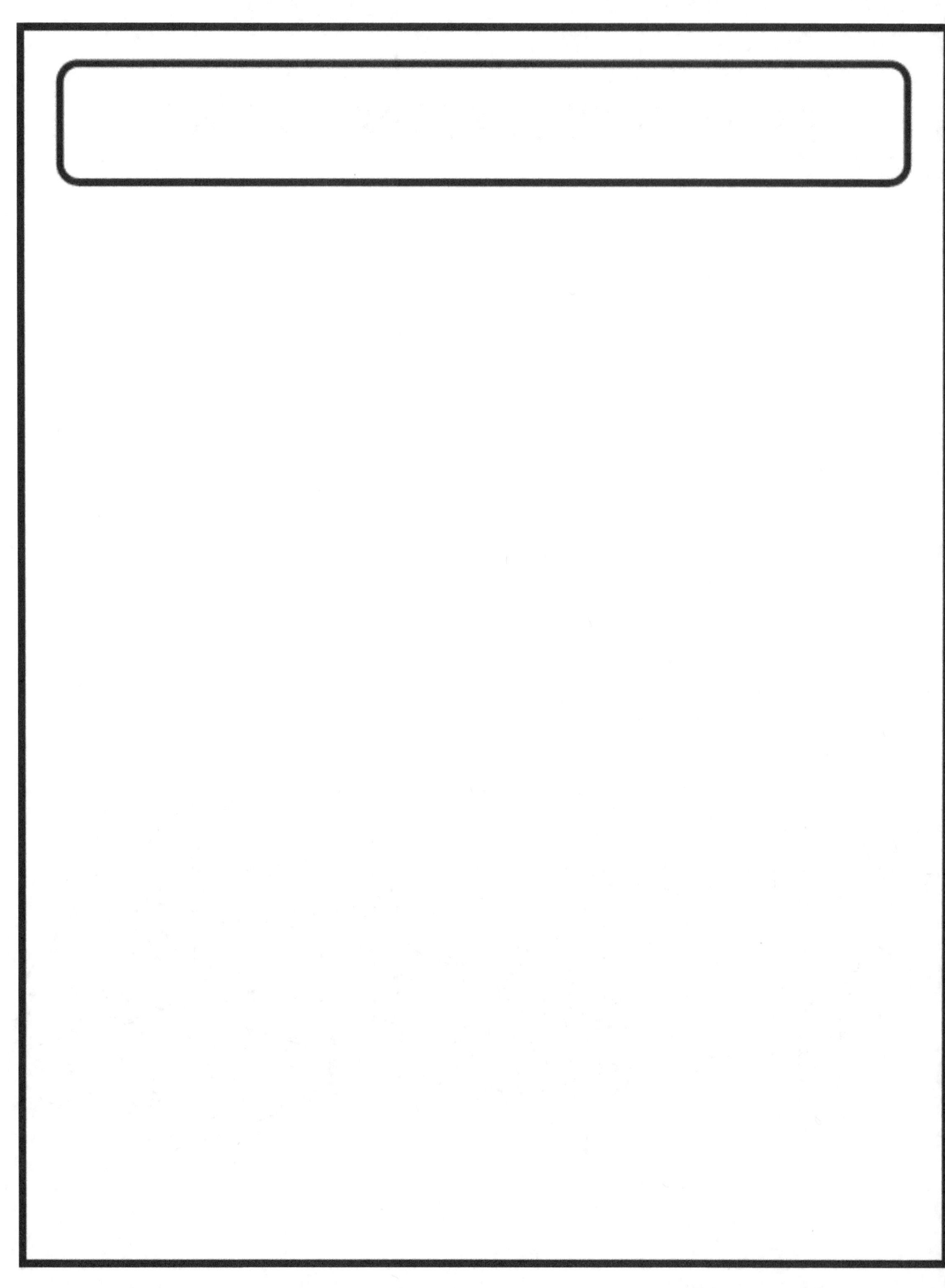

SKYSCRAPERS COLORING BOOK

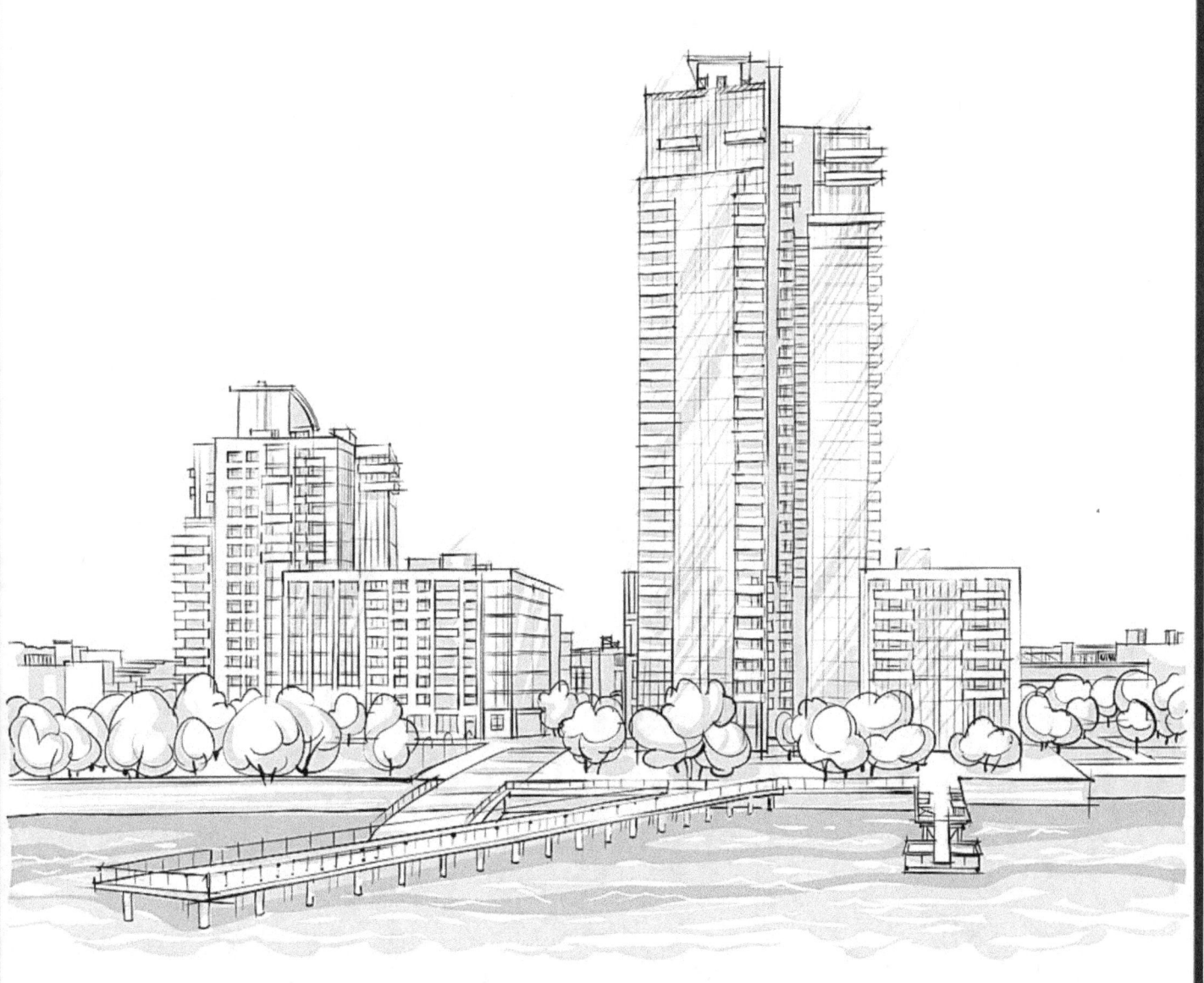

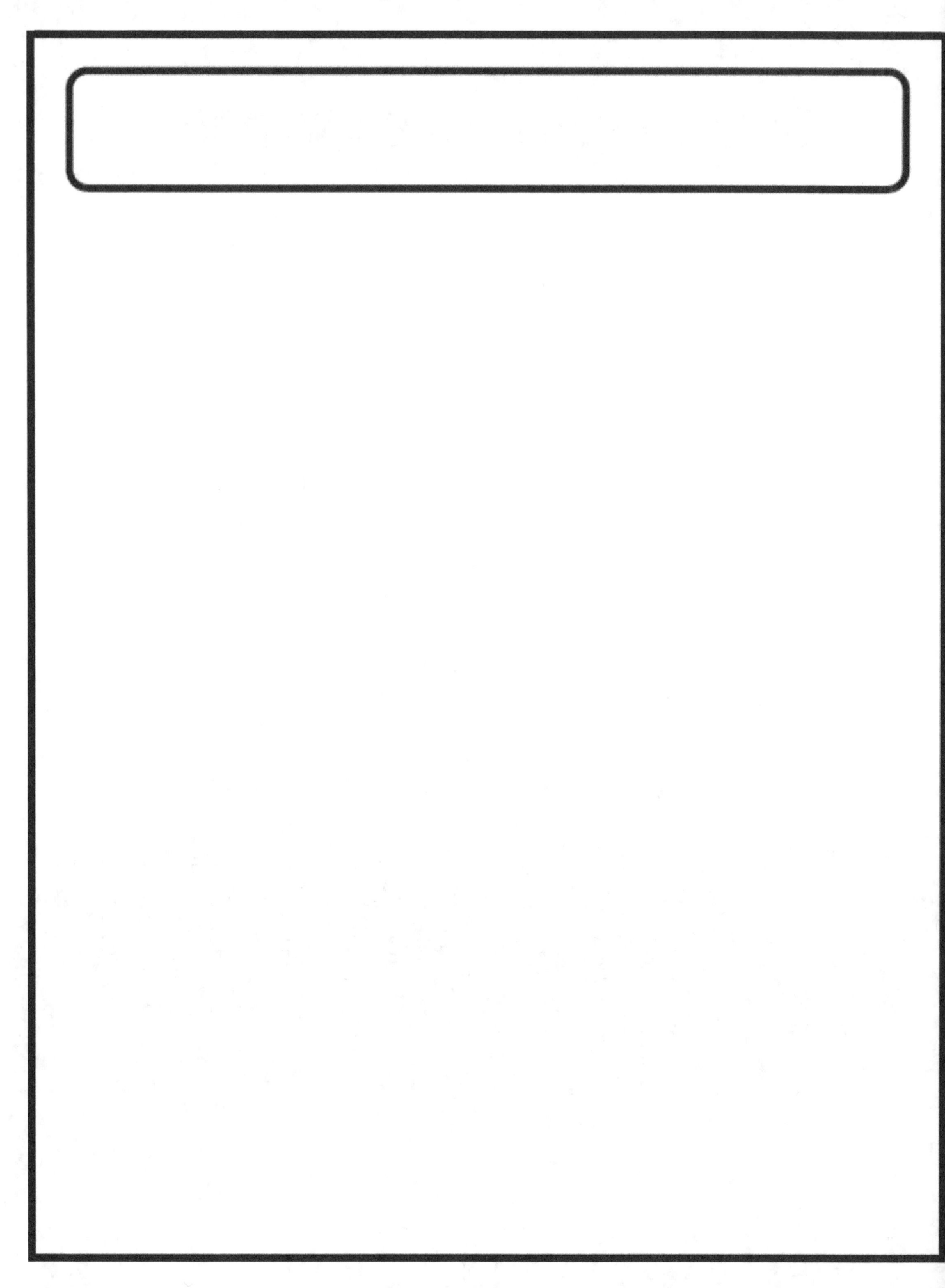

SKYSCRAPERS COLORING BOOK

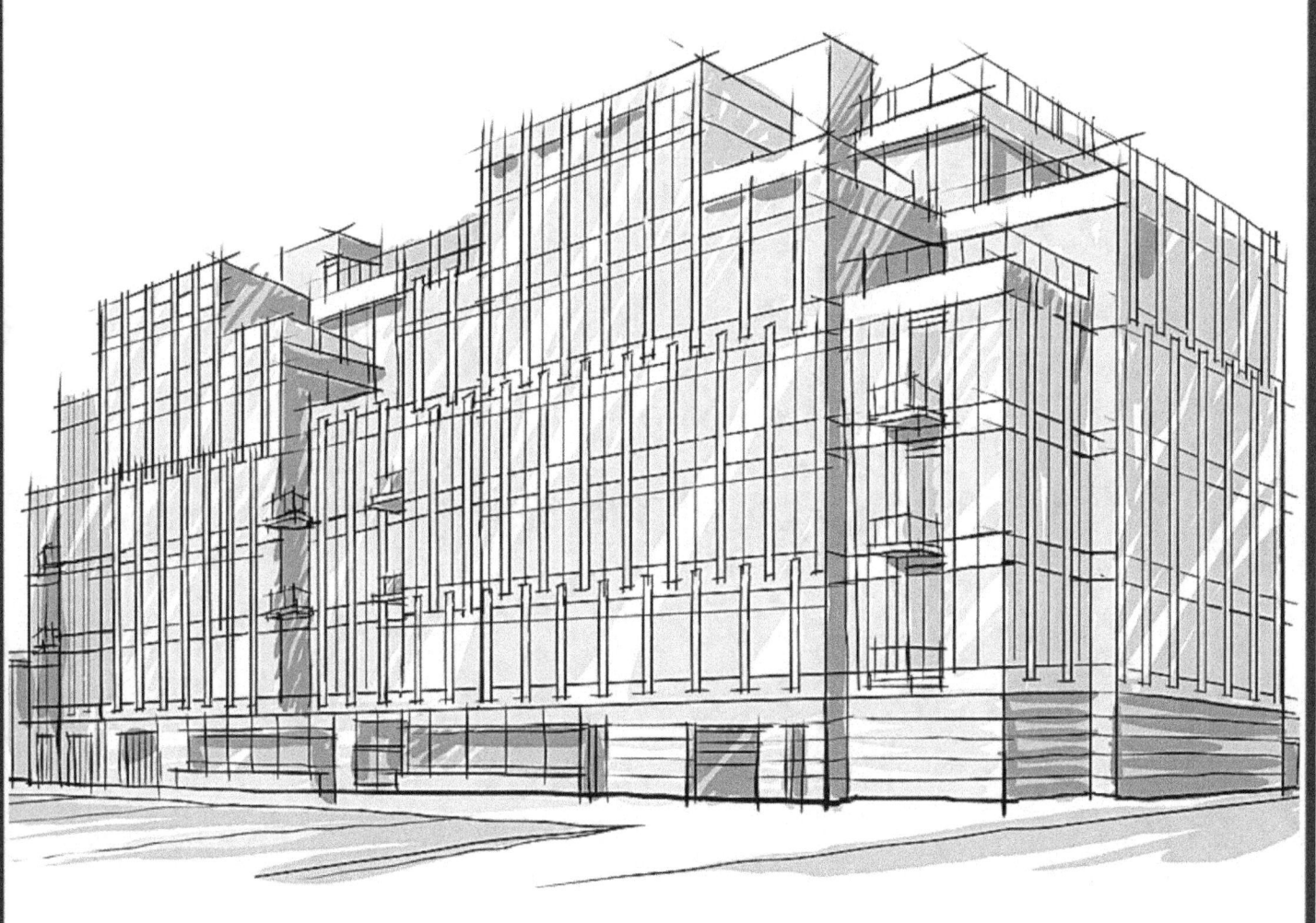

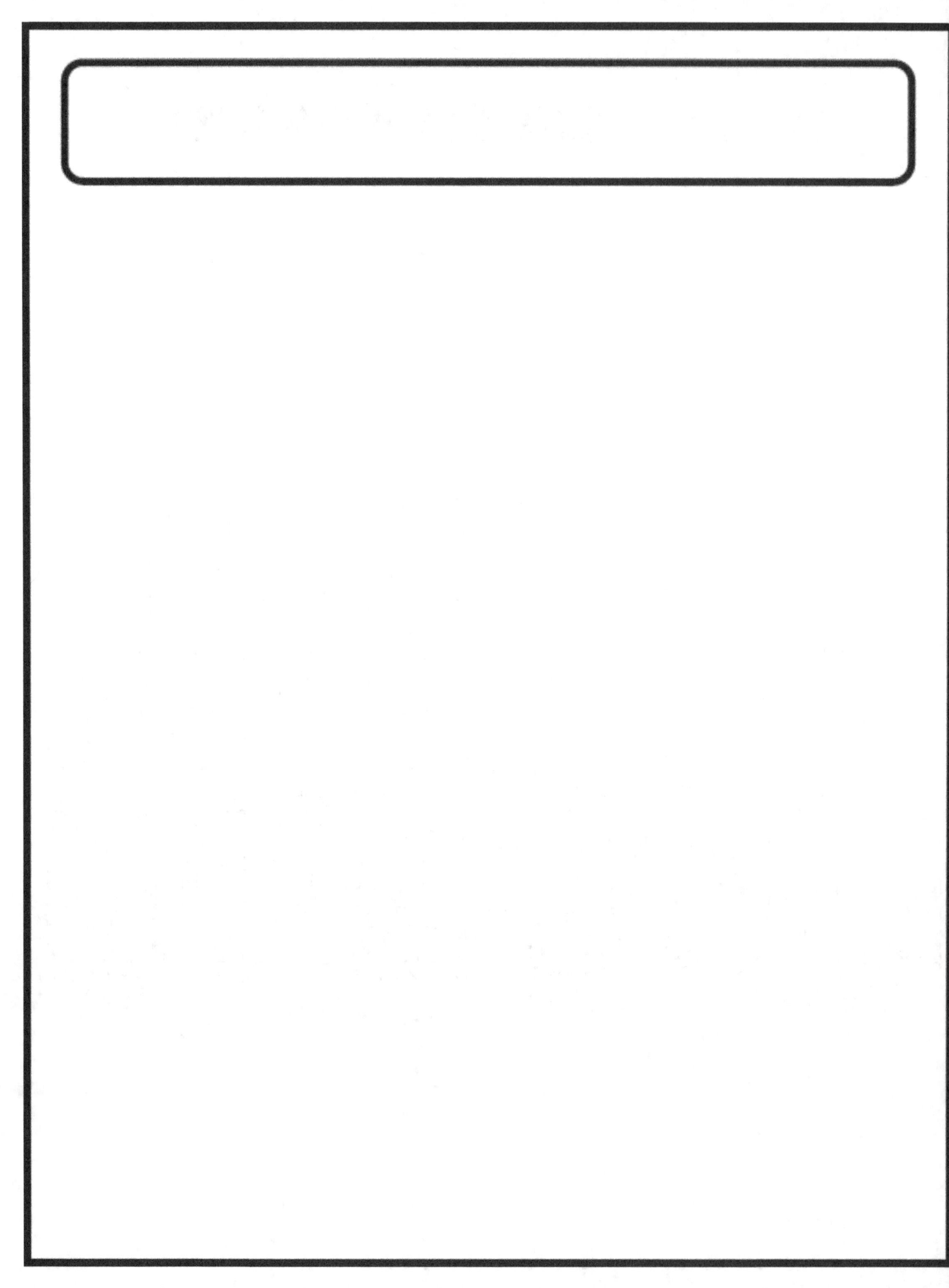

SKYSCRAPERS COLORING BOOK

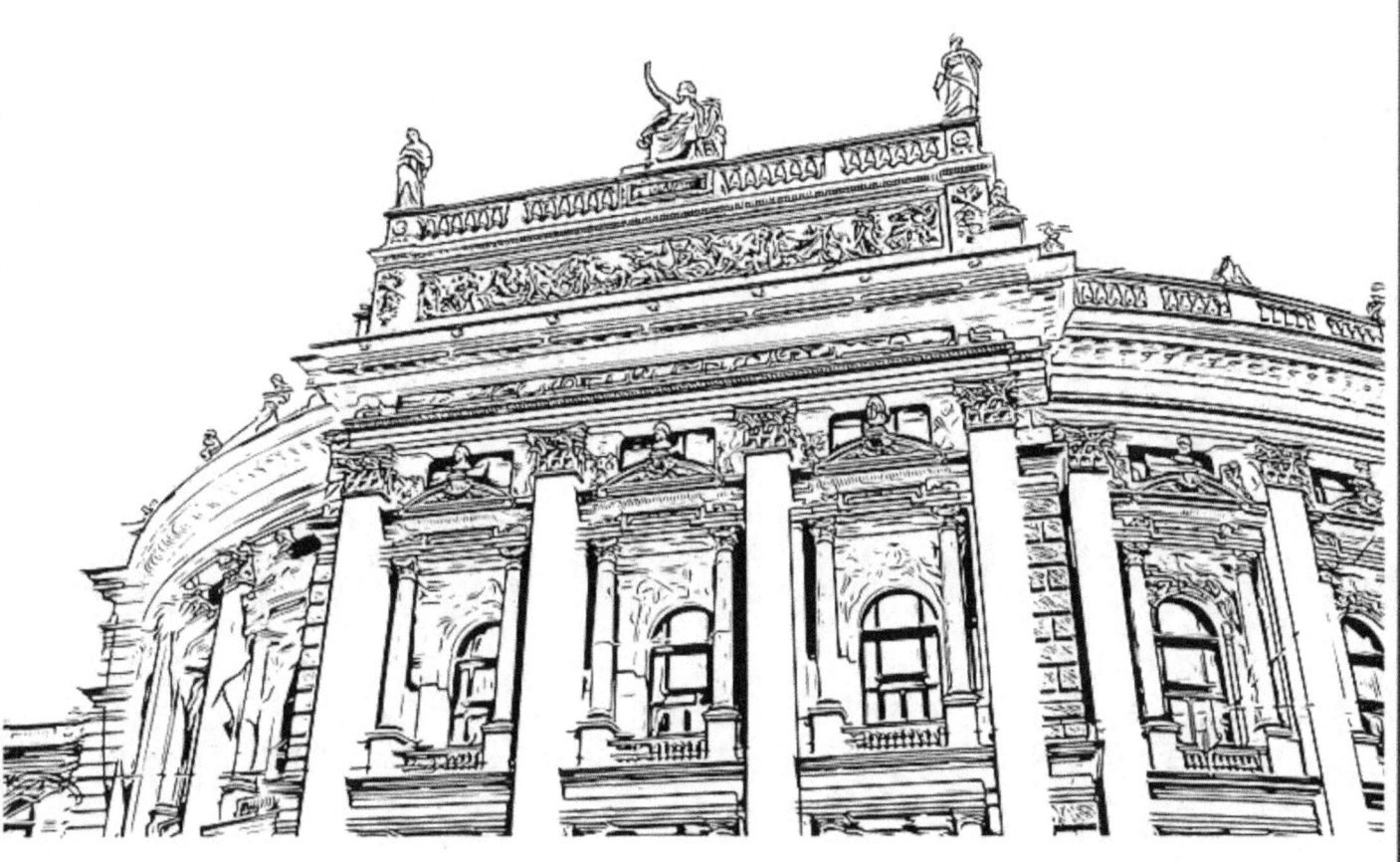

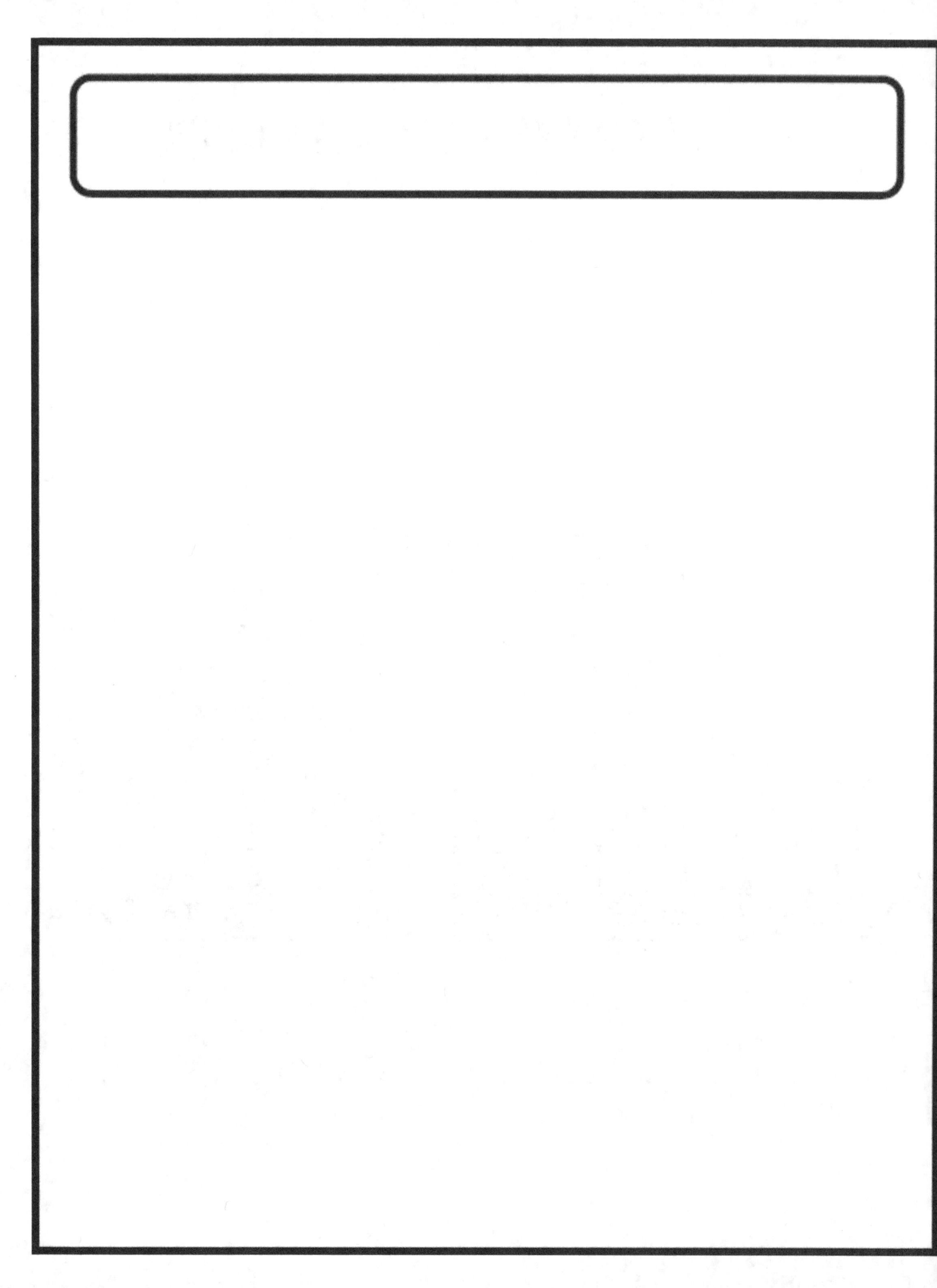

SKYSCRAPERS COLORING BOOK

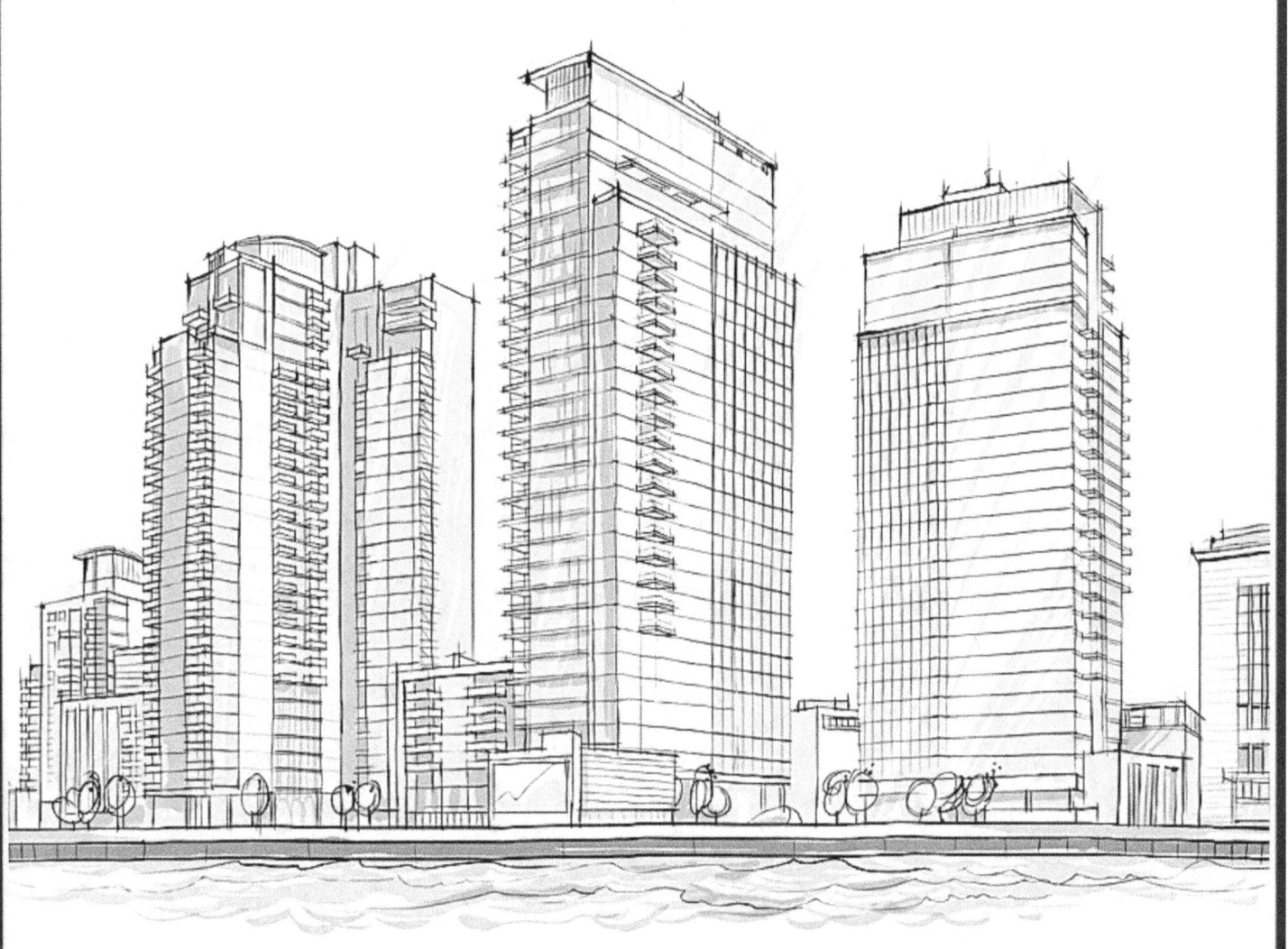

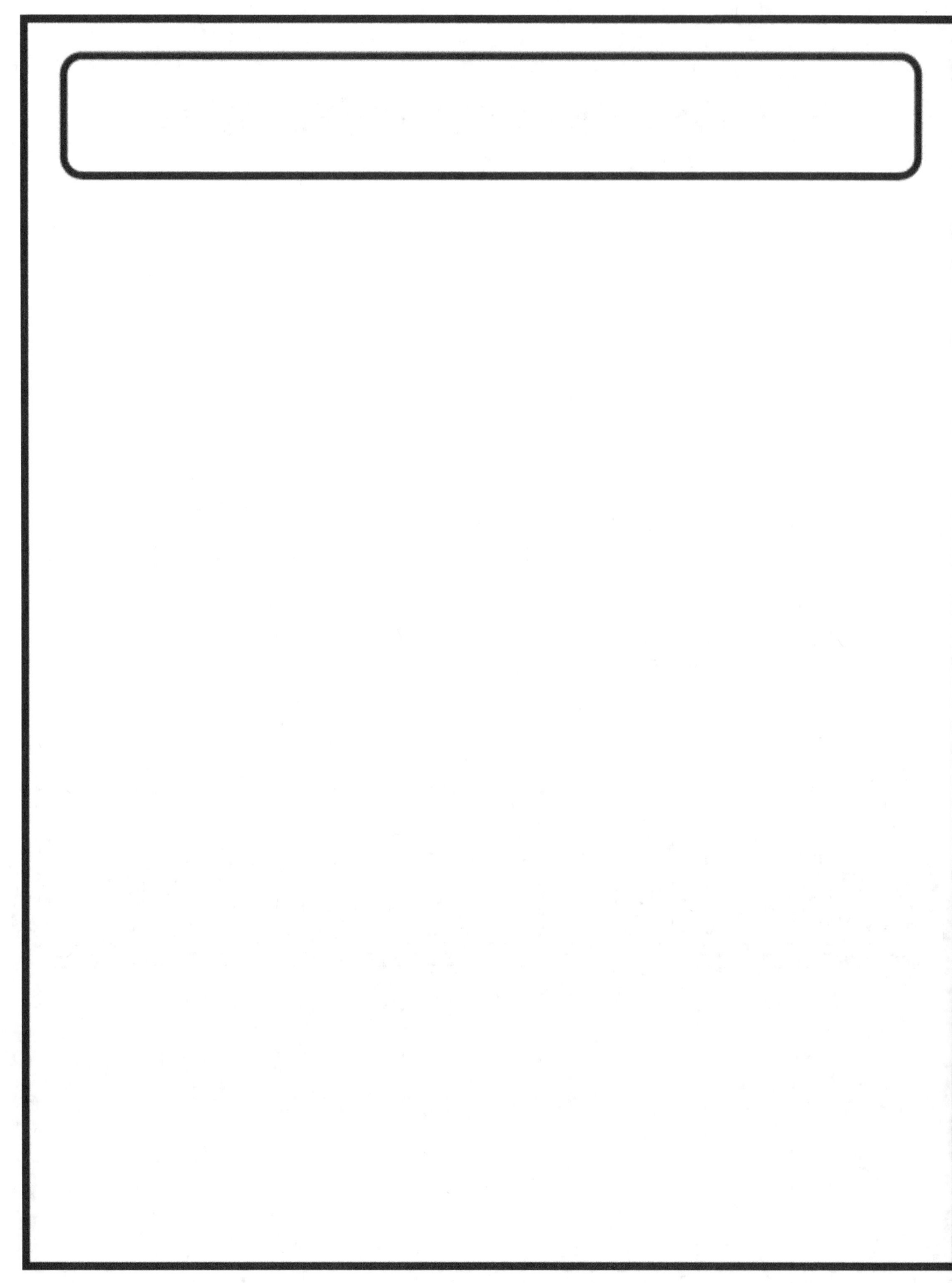

SKYSCRAPERS COLORING BOOK

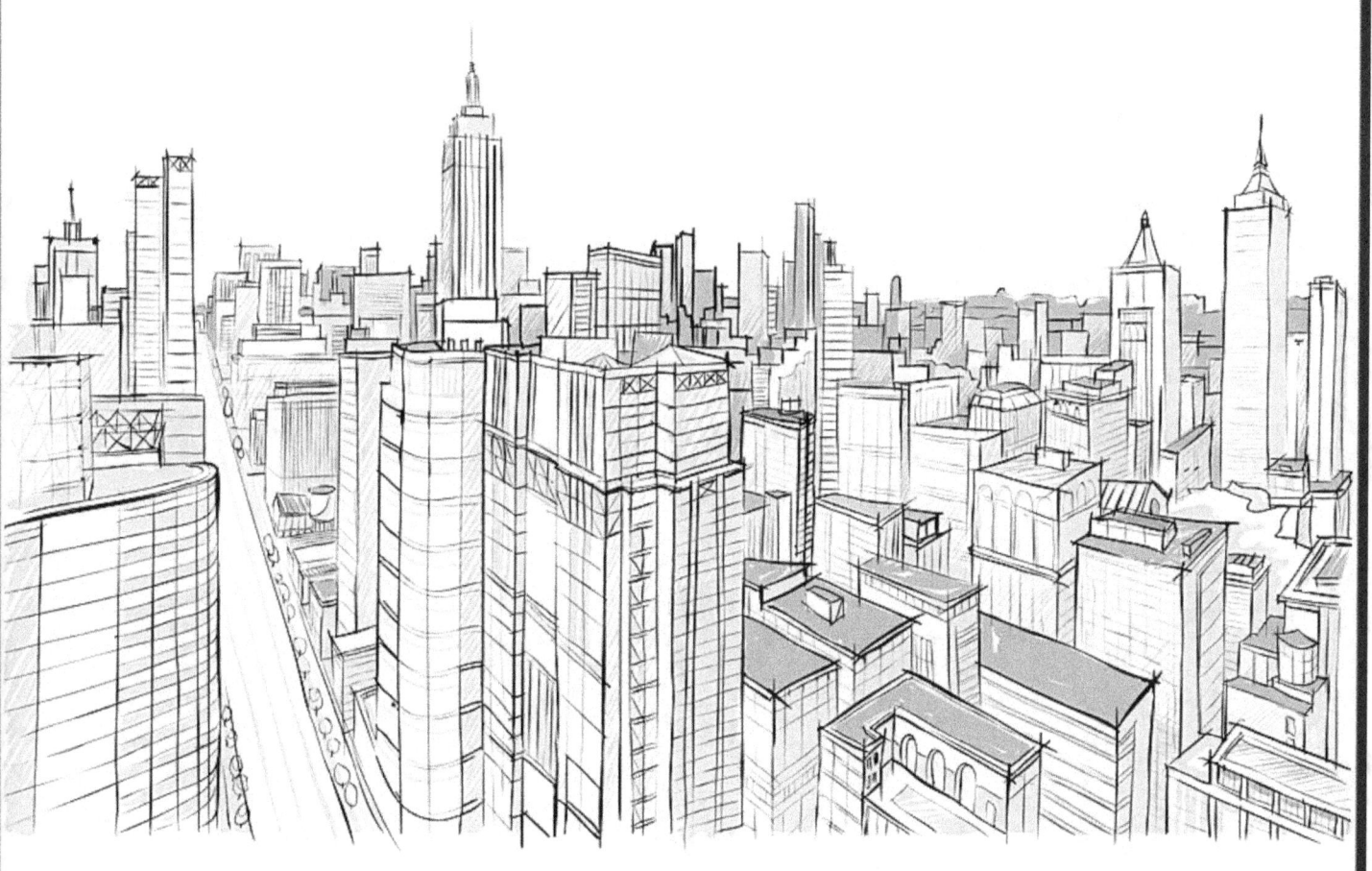

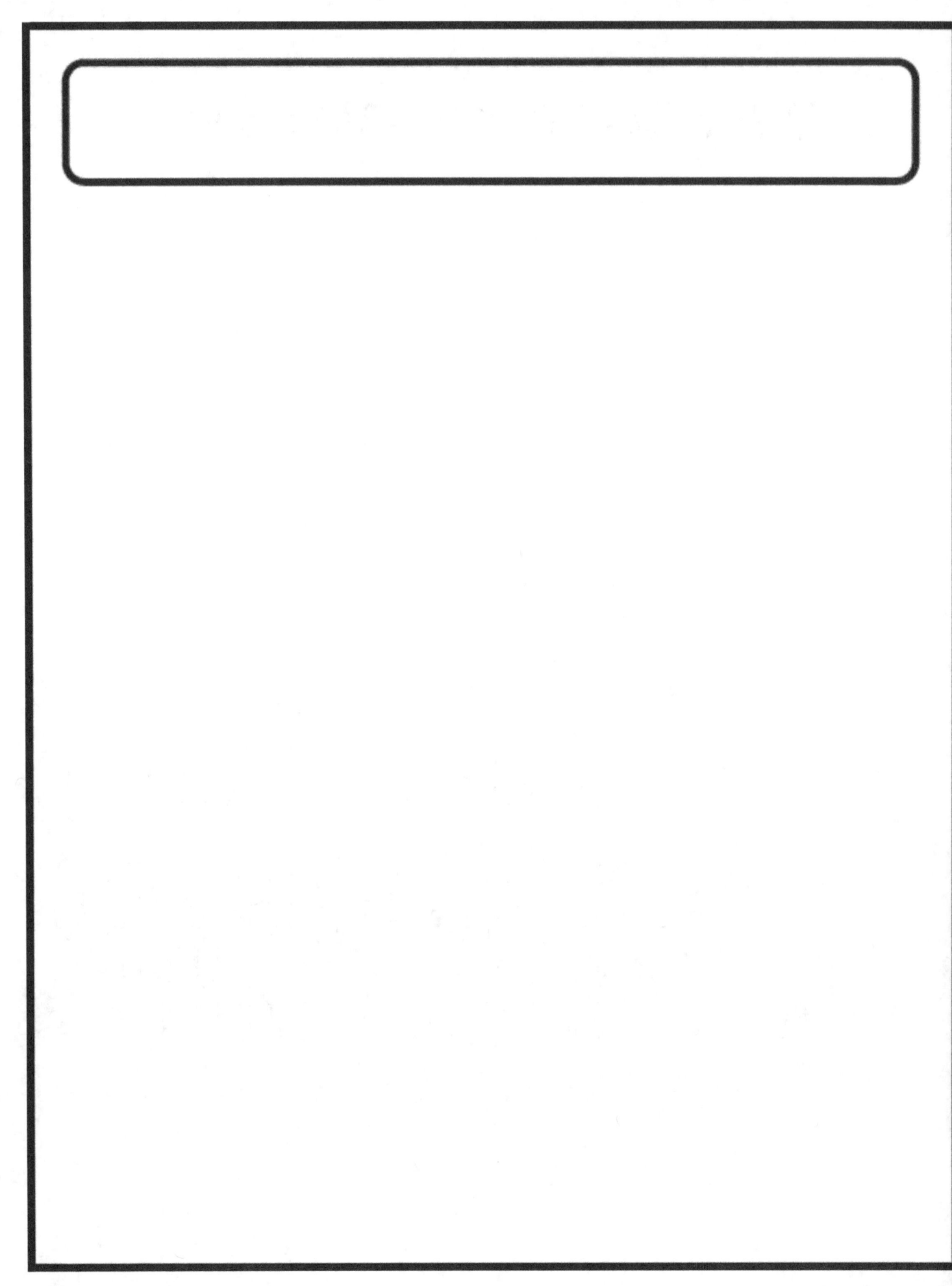

SKYSCRAPERS COLORING BOOK

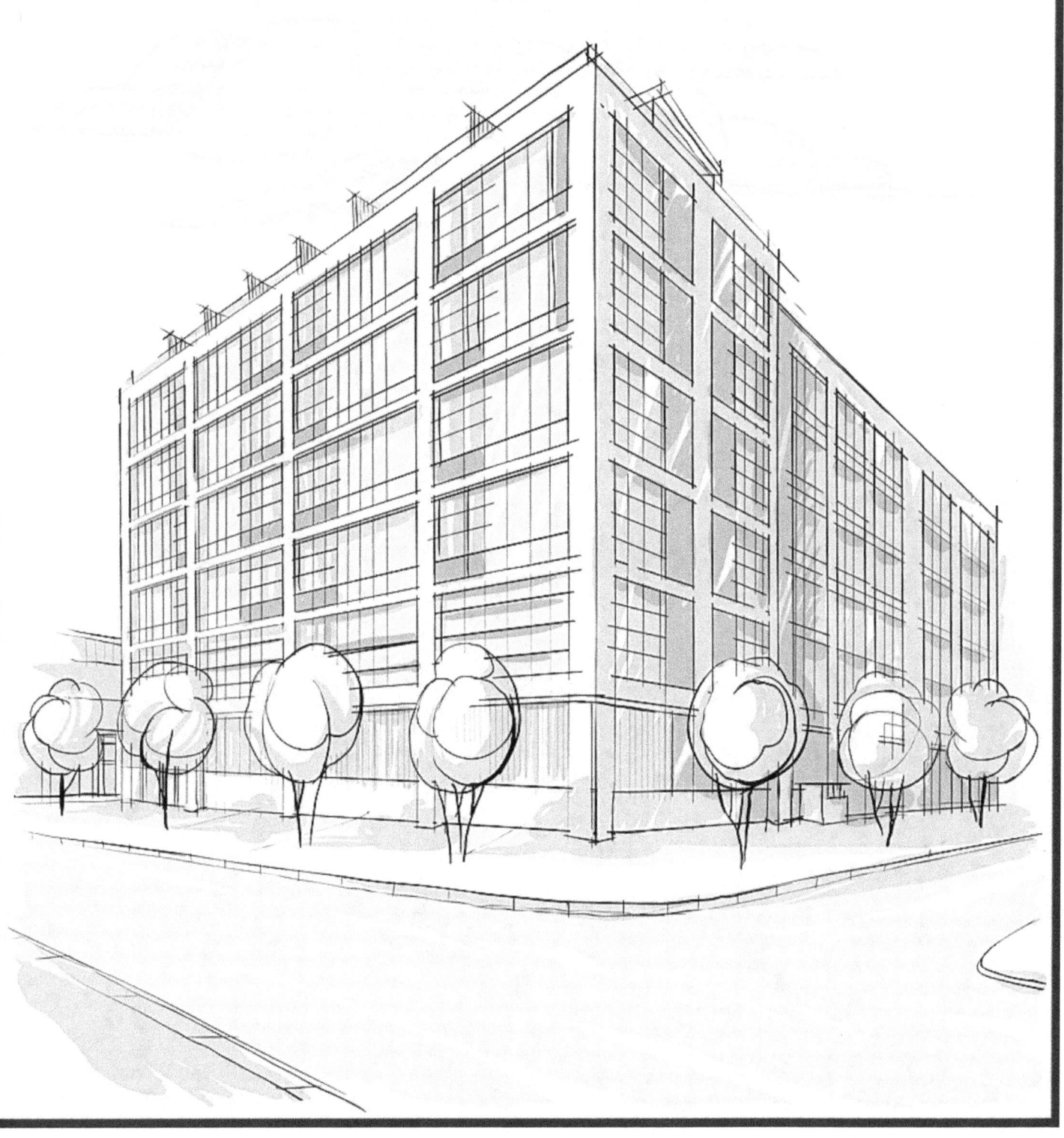

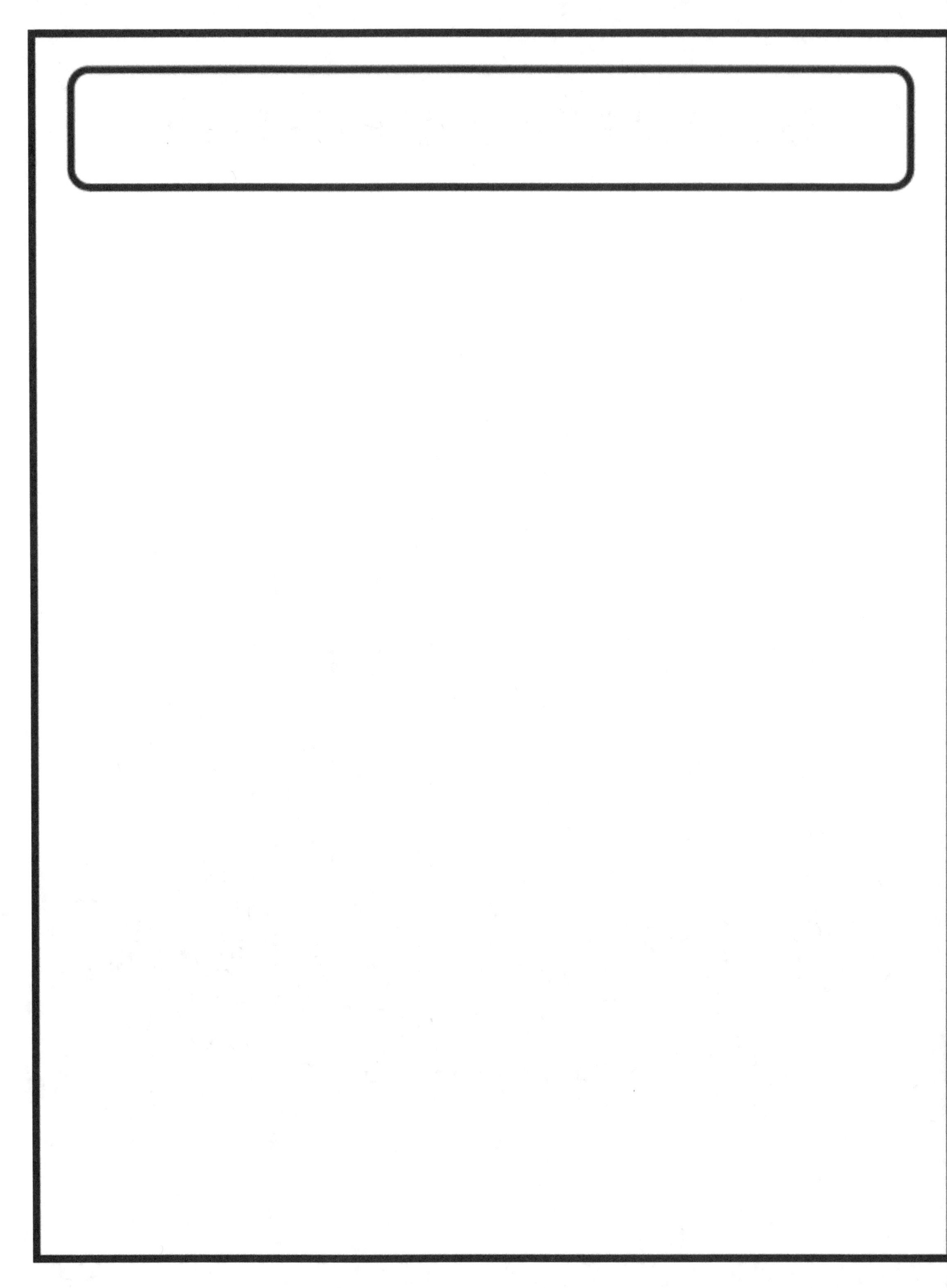

SKYSCRAPERS COLORING BOOK

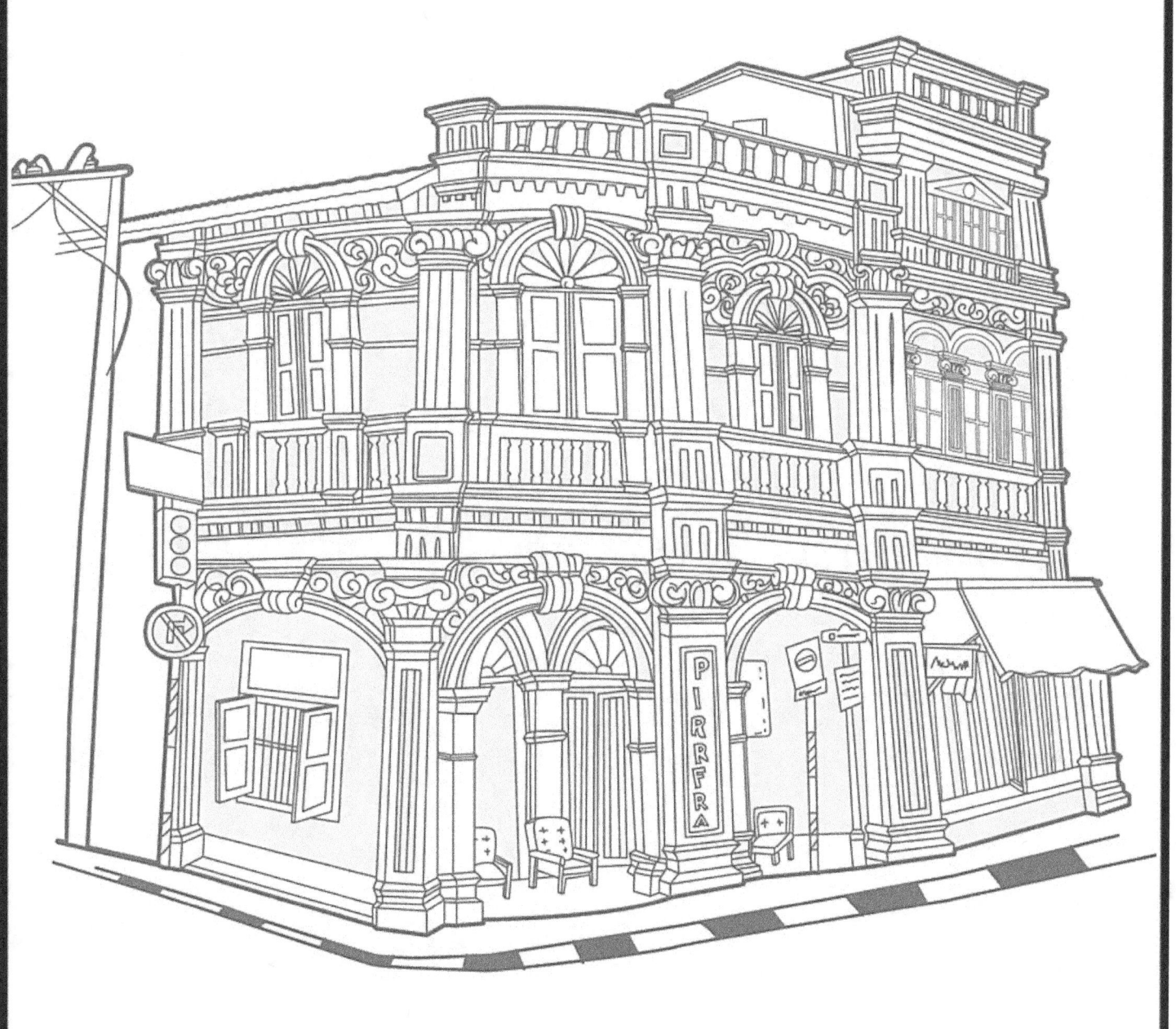

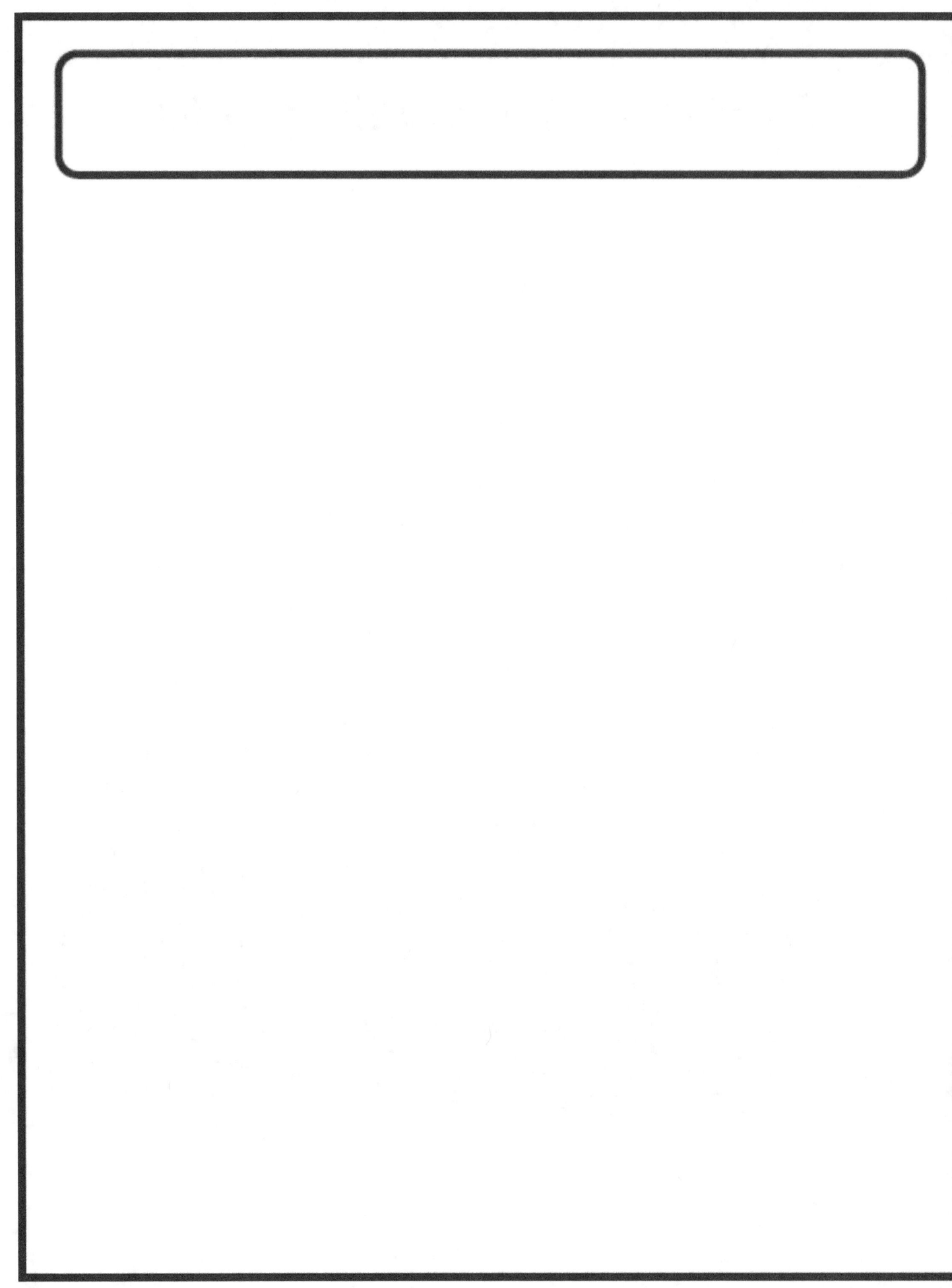

SKYSCRAPERS COLORING BOOK

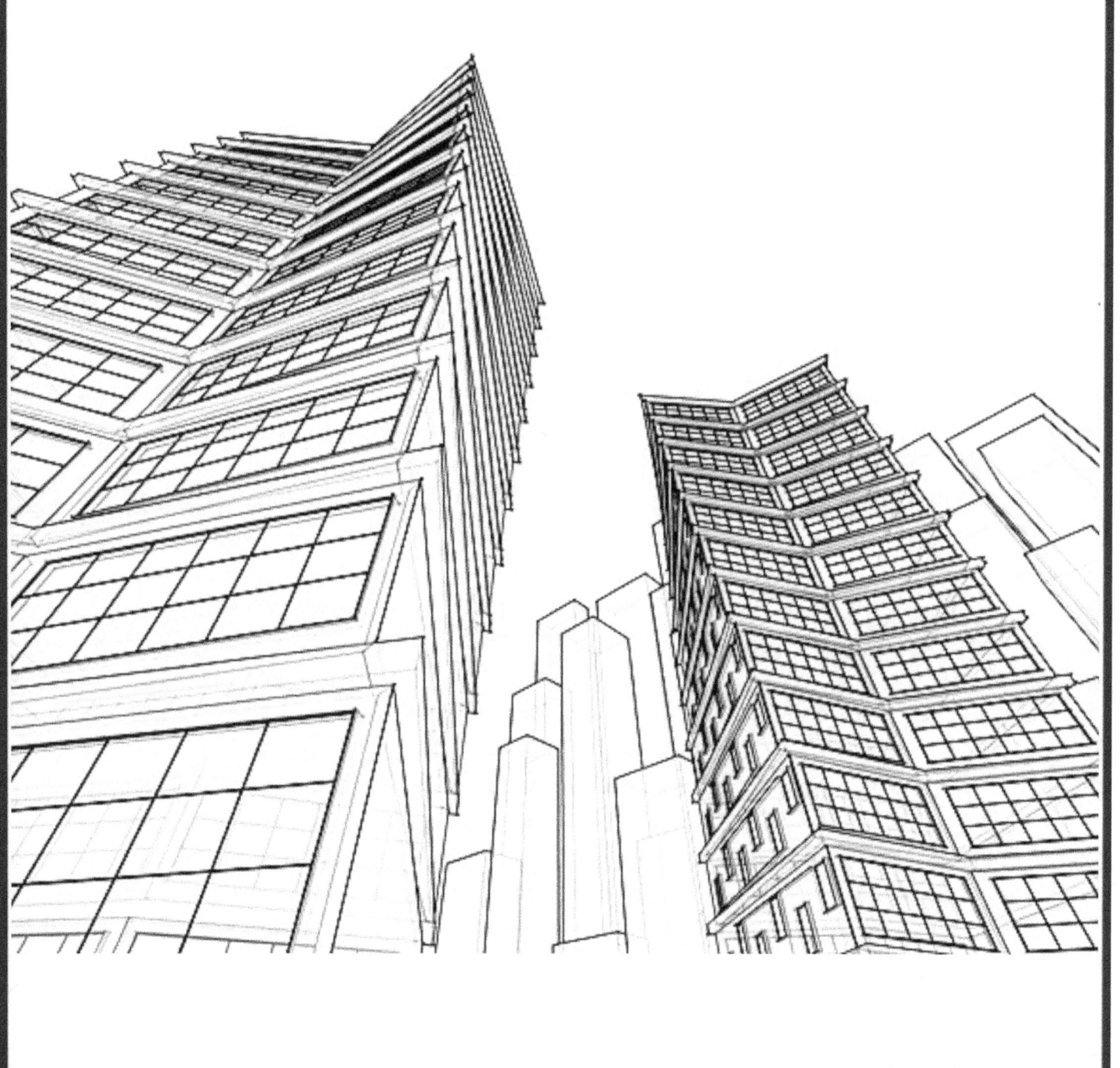

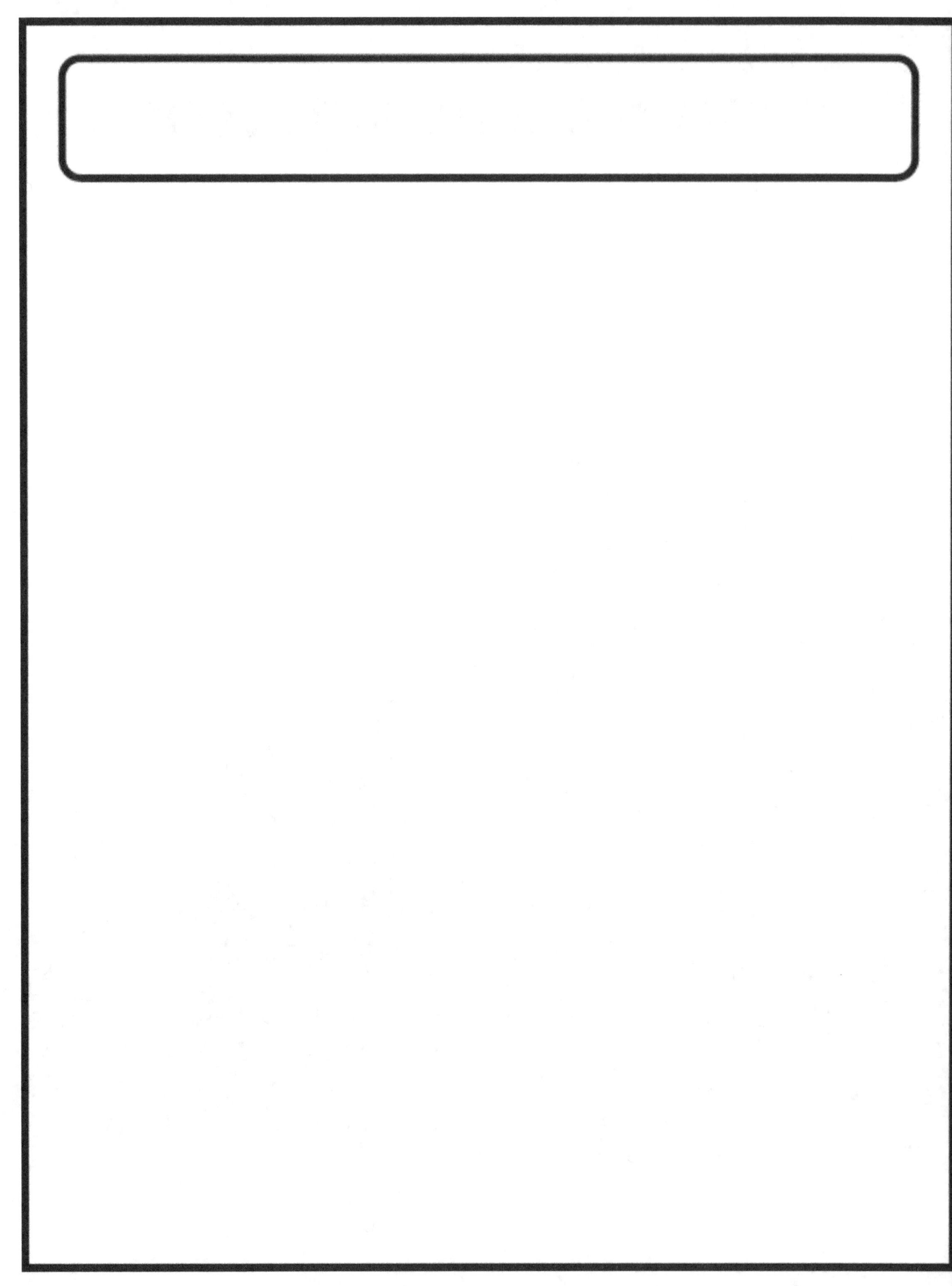

SKYSCRAPERS COLORING BOOK

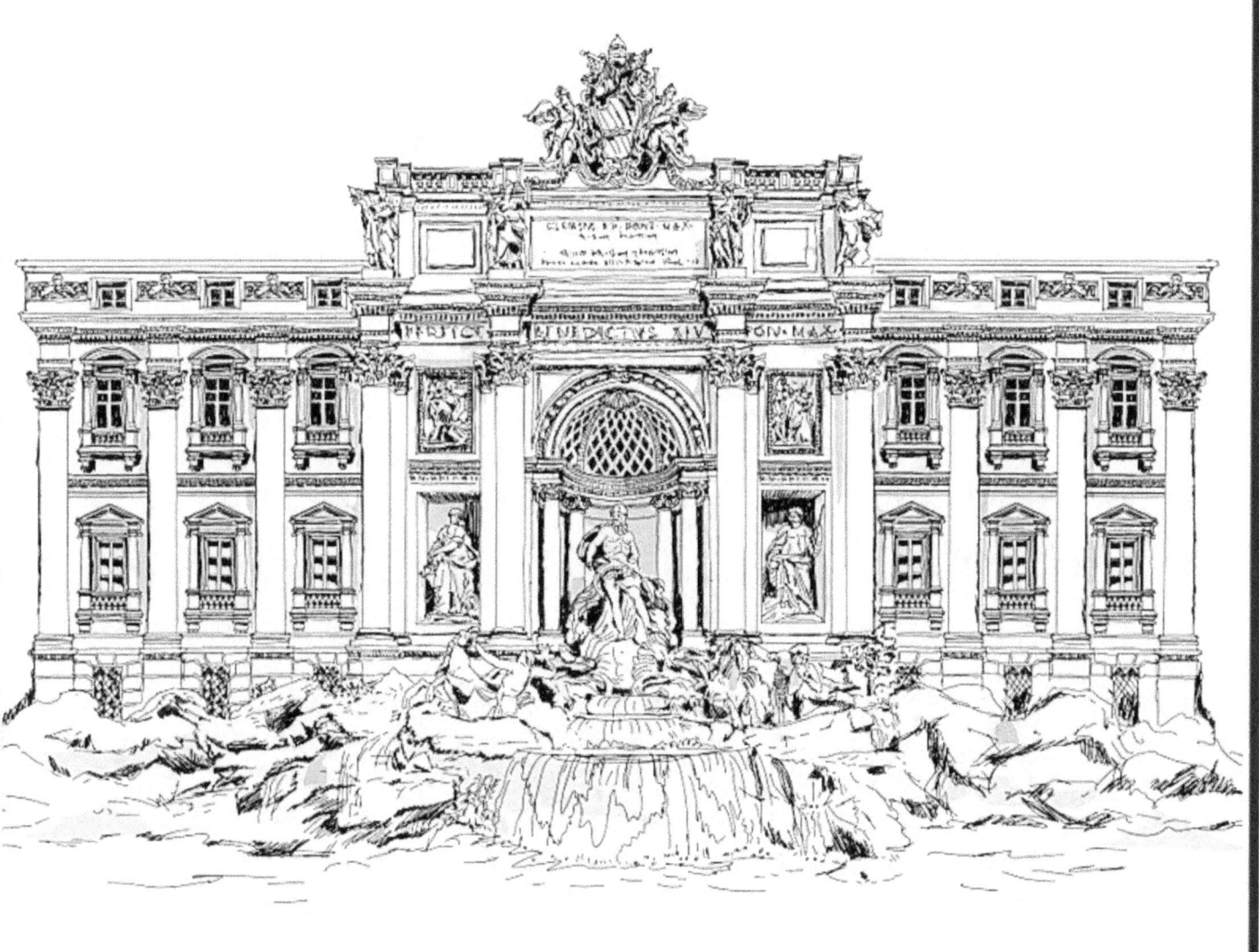

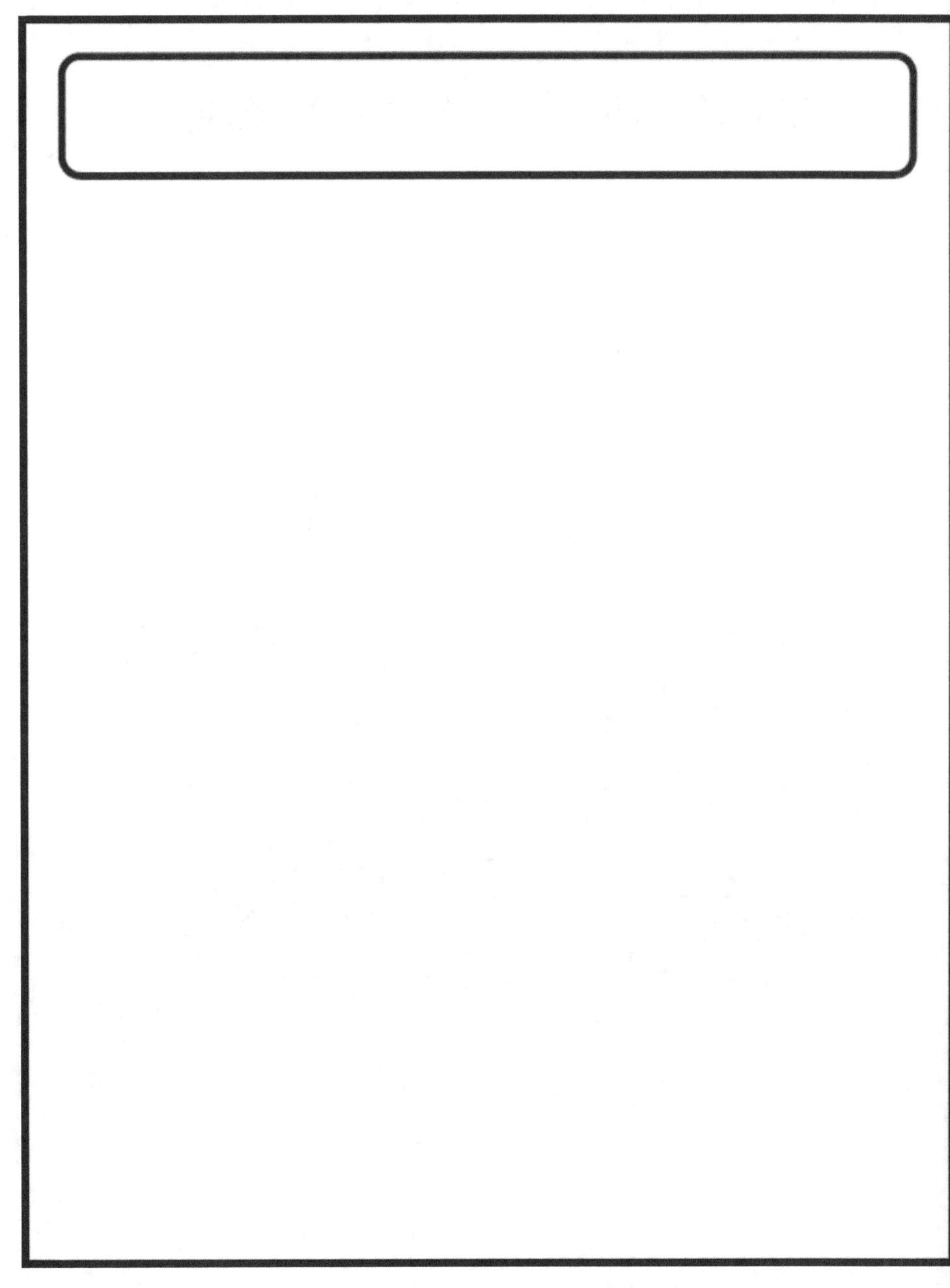

SKYSCRAPERS COLORING BOOK

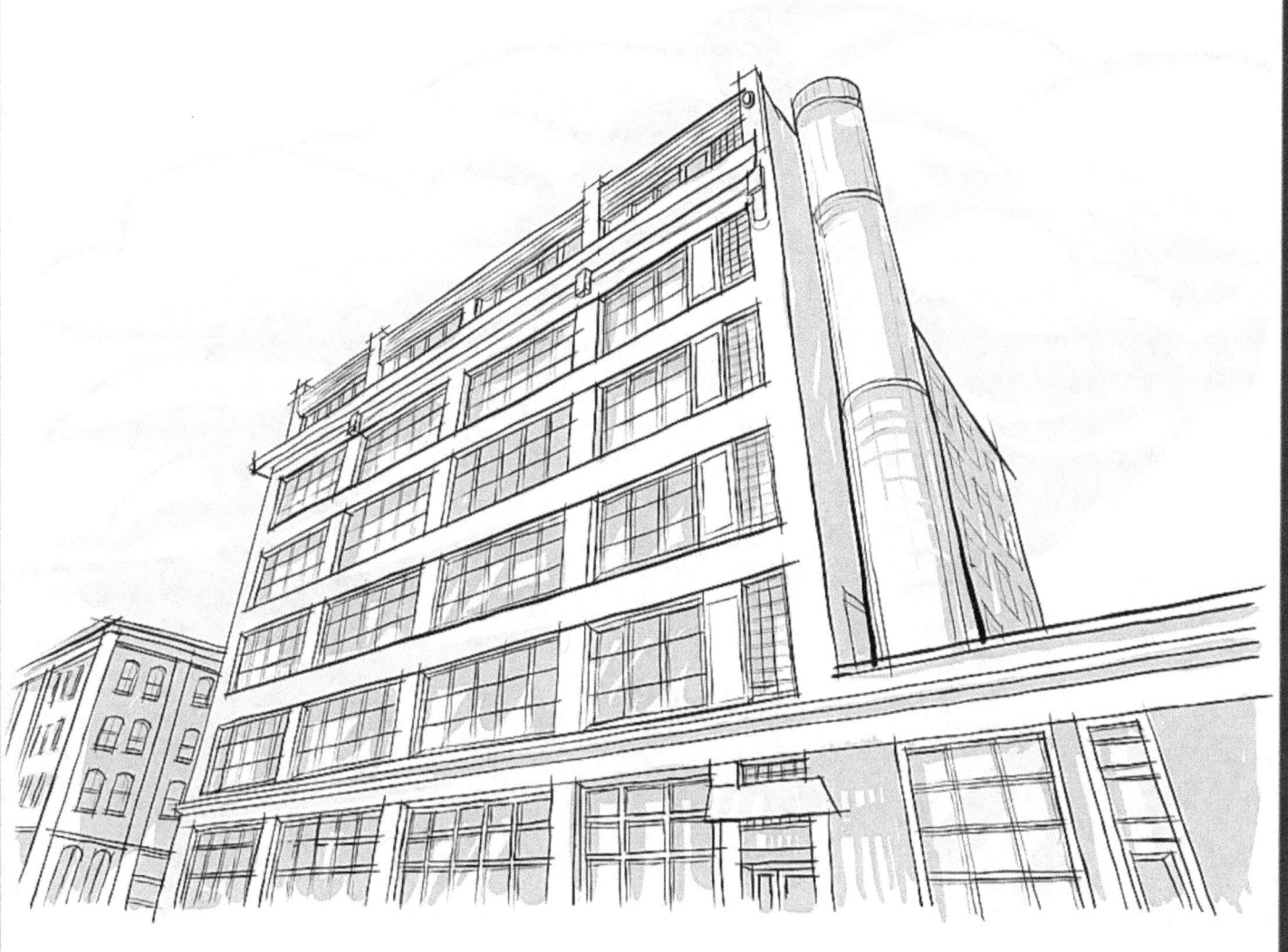

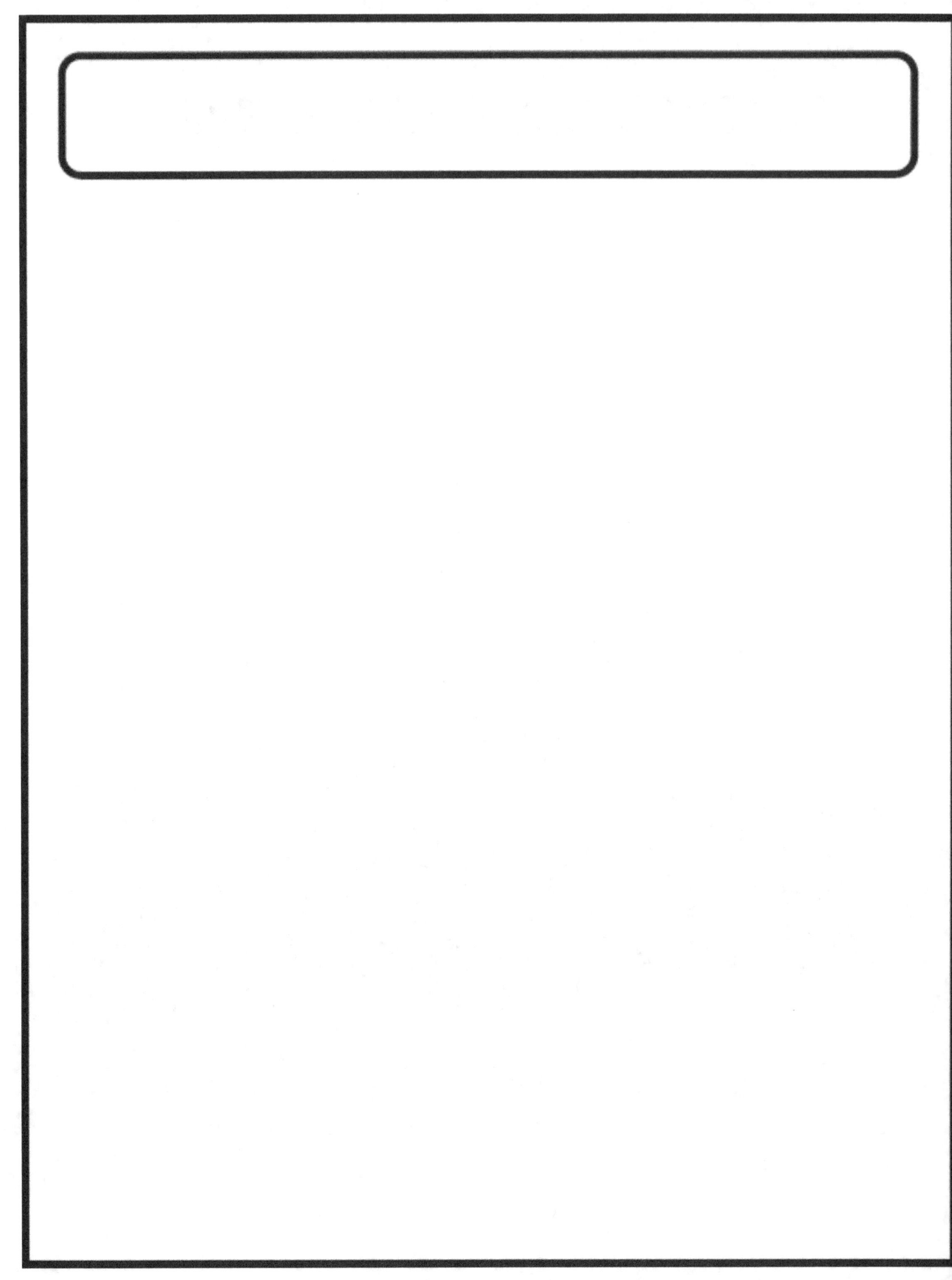

SKYSCRAPERS COLORING BOOK

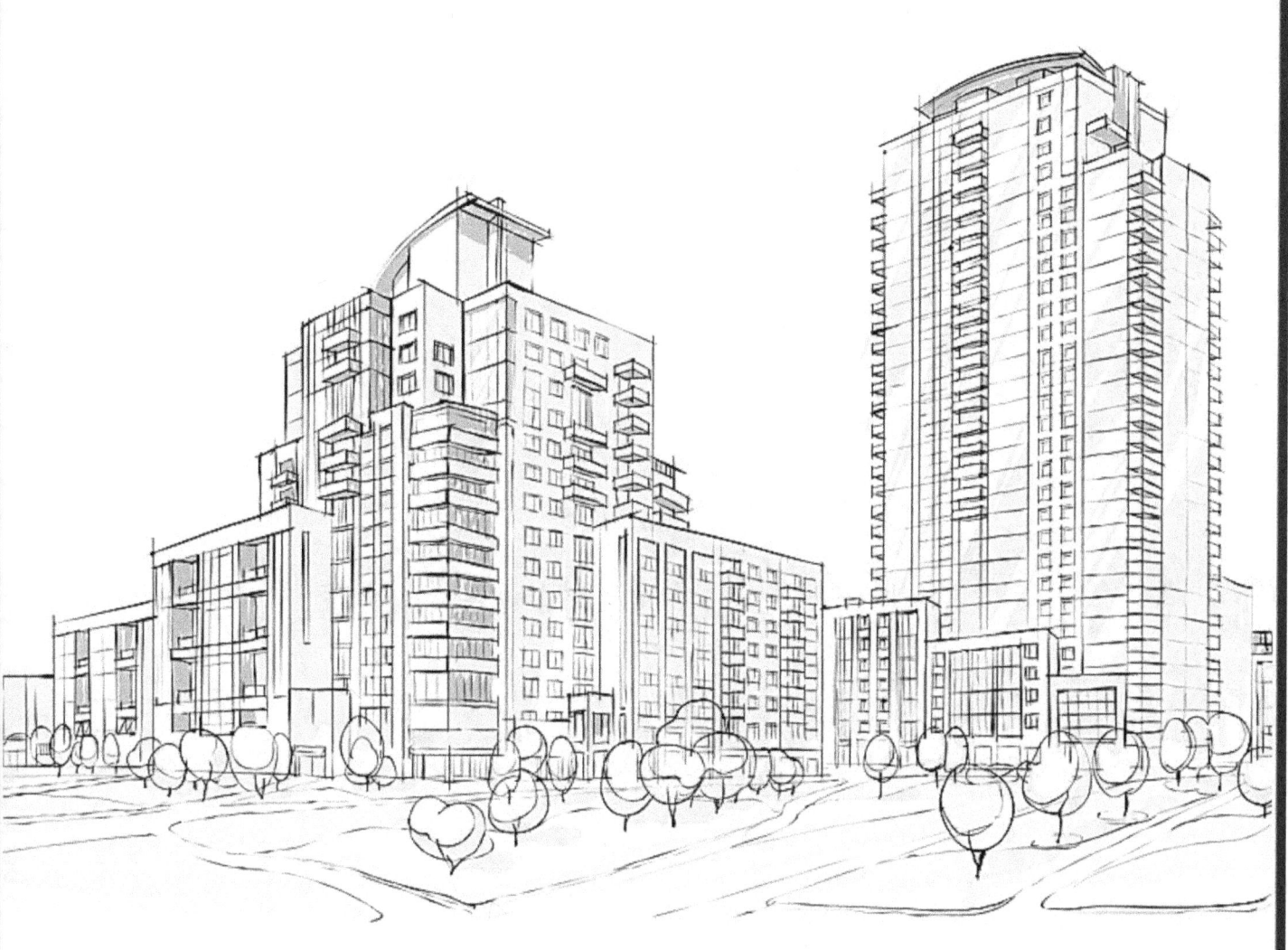

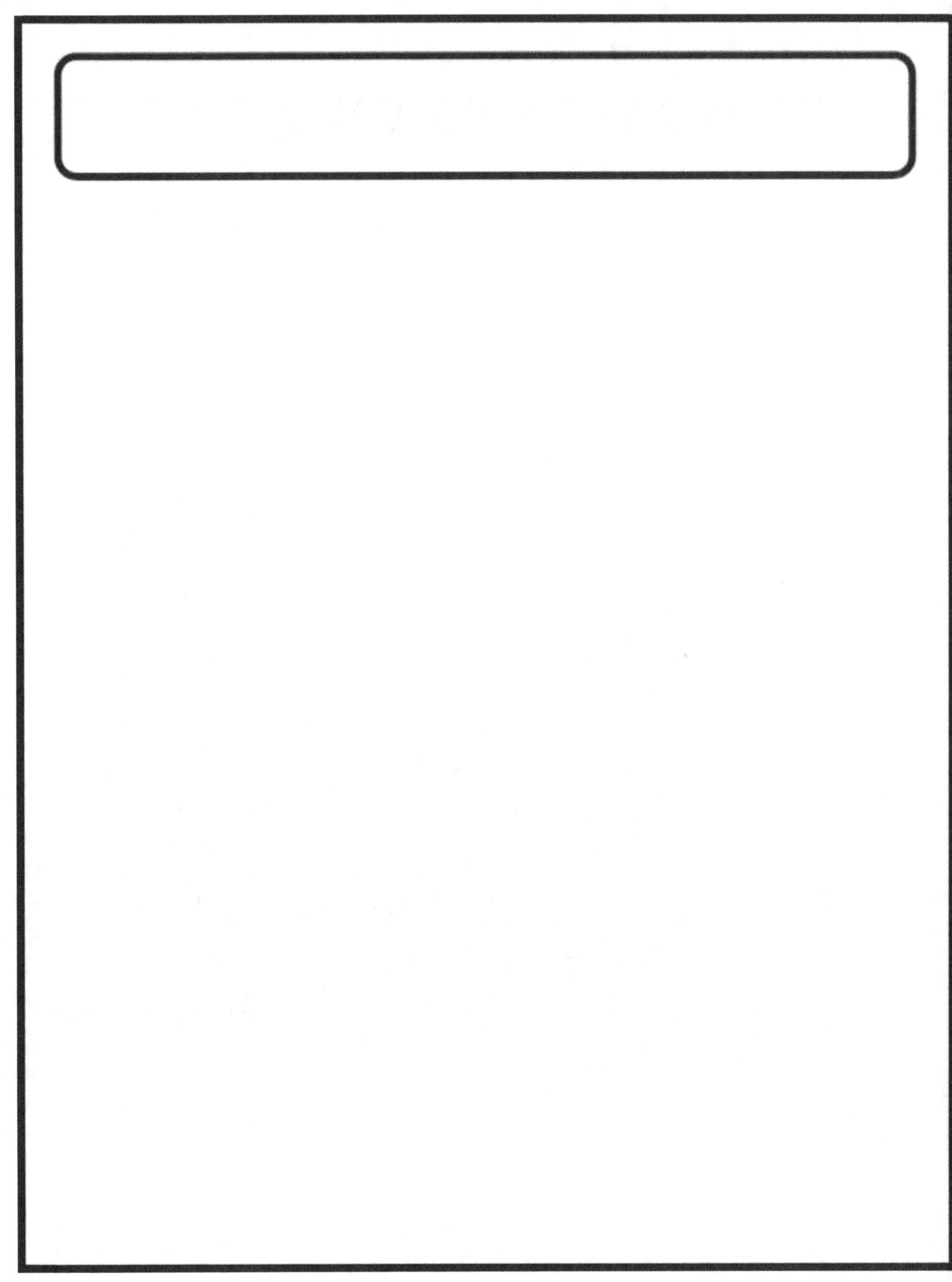

SKYSCRAPERS COLORING BOOK

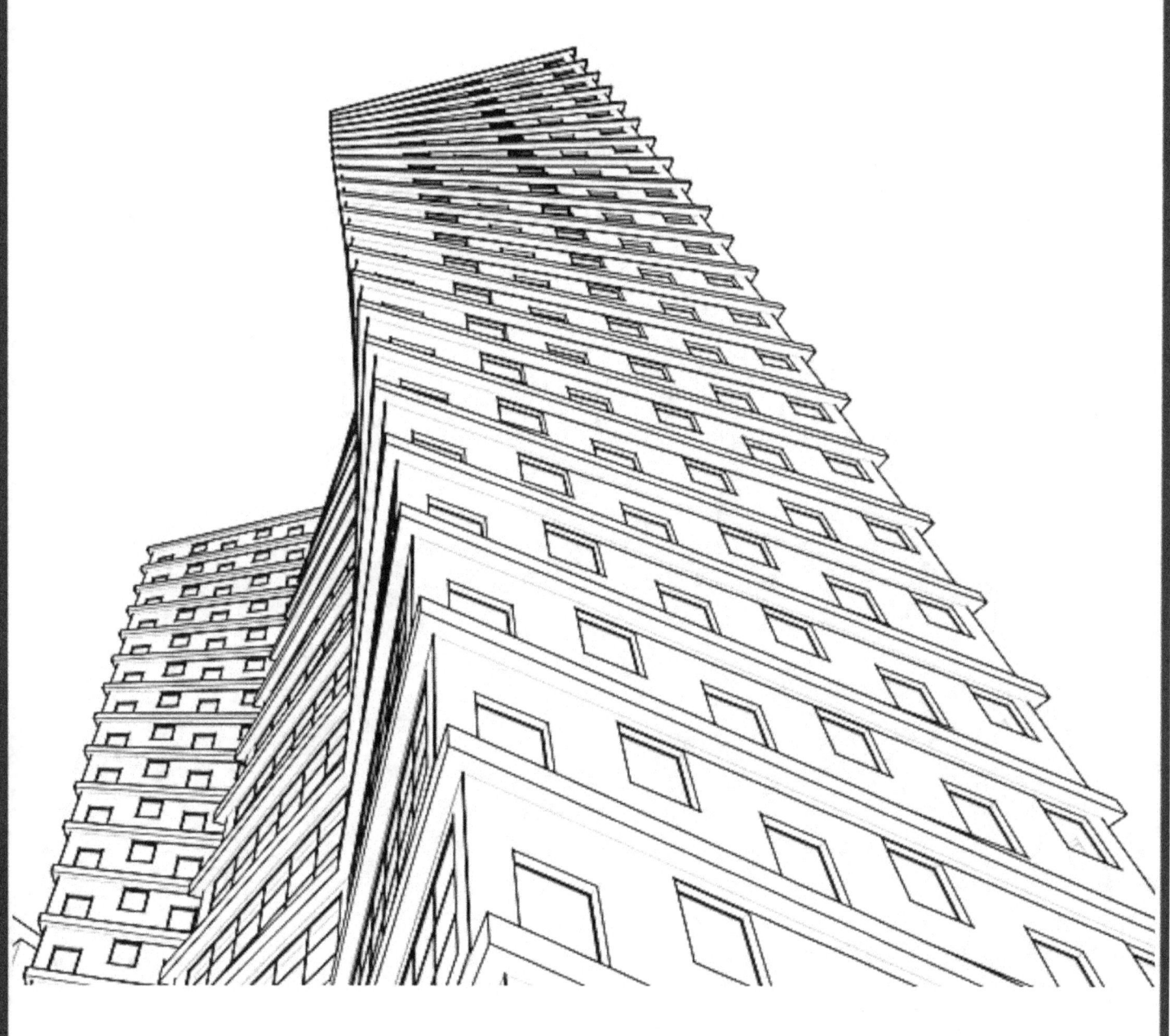

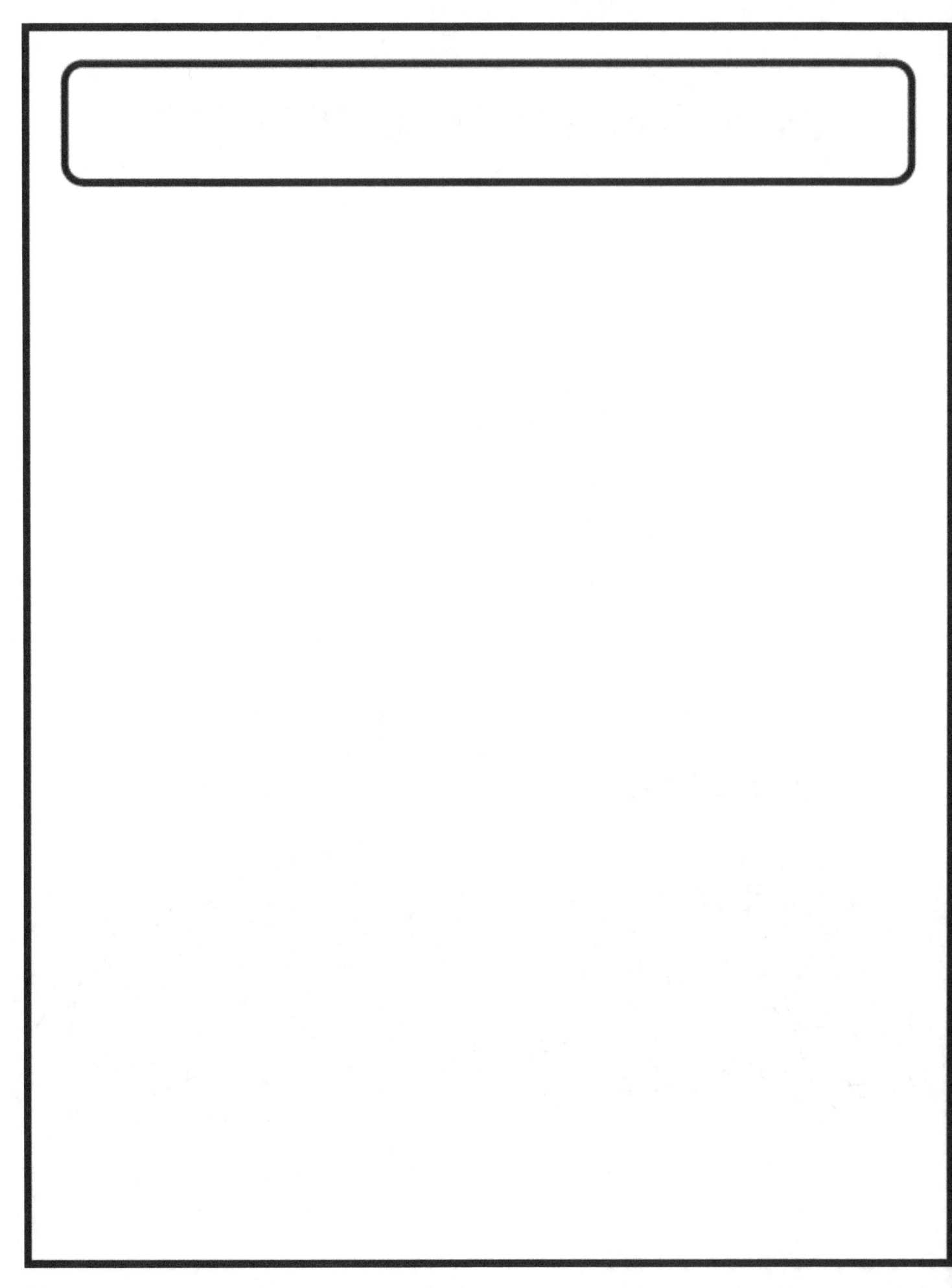

SKYSCRAPERS COLORING BOOK

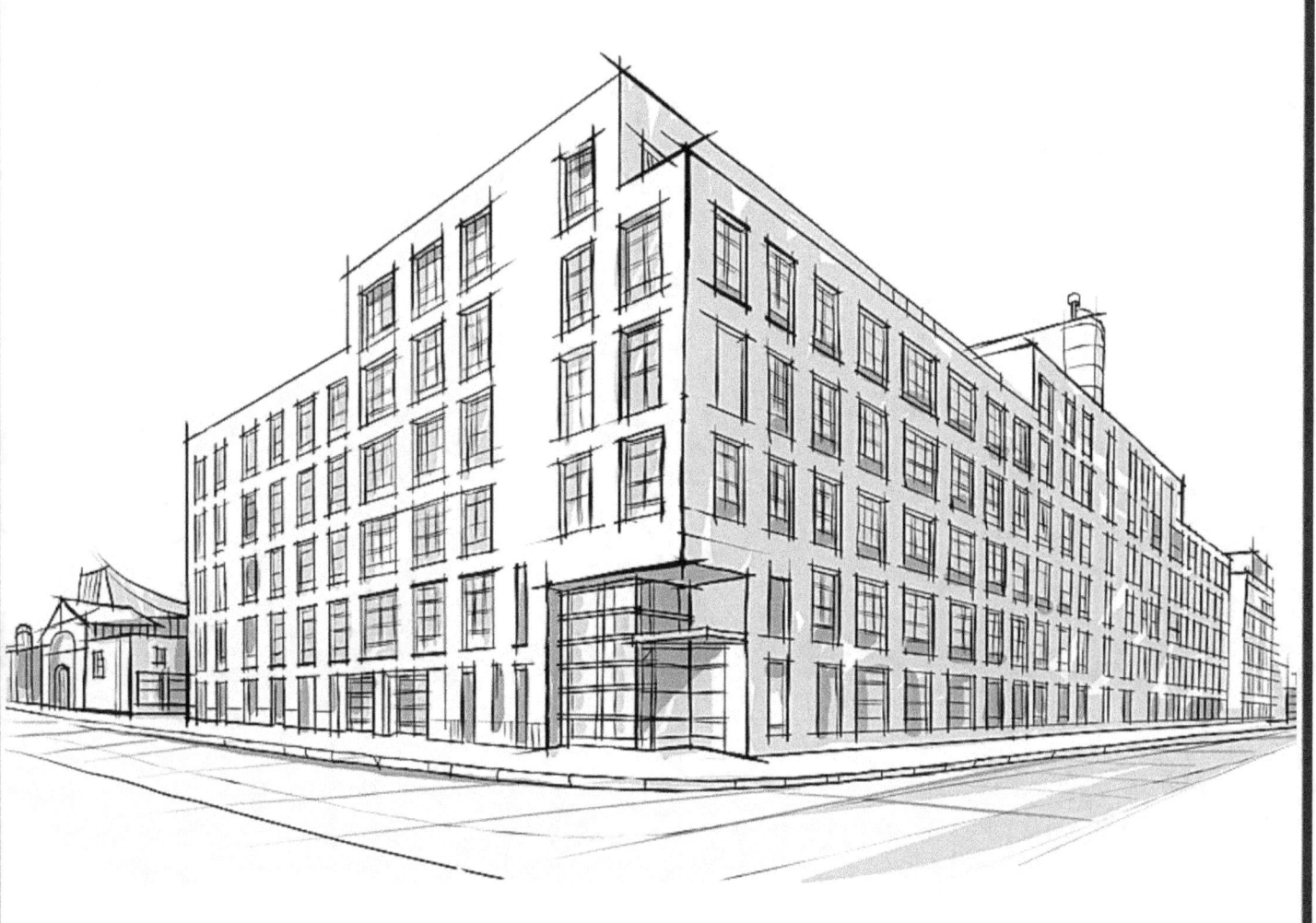

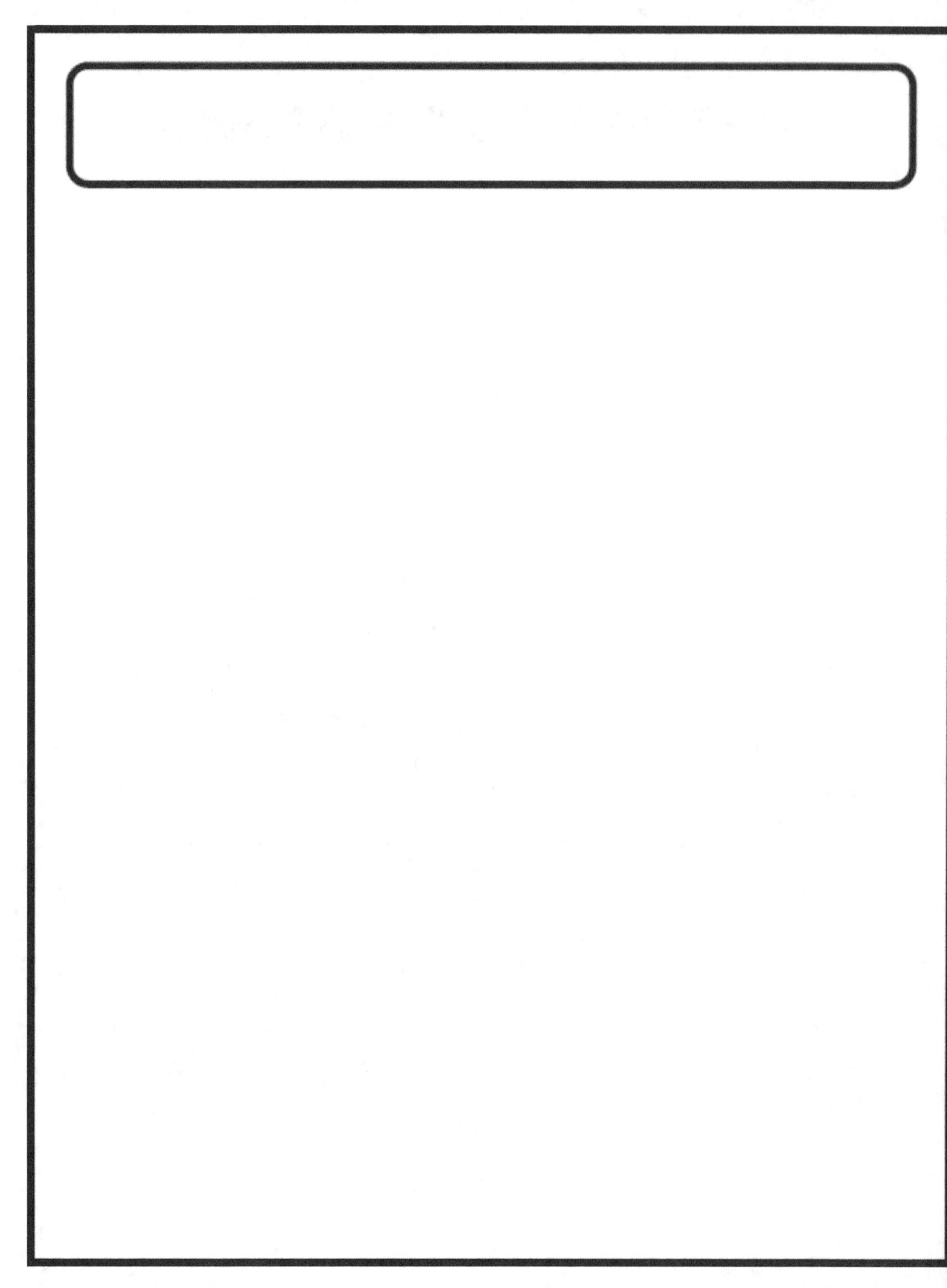

SKYSCRAPERS COLORING BOOK

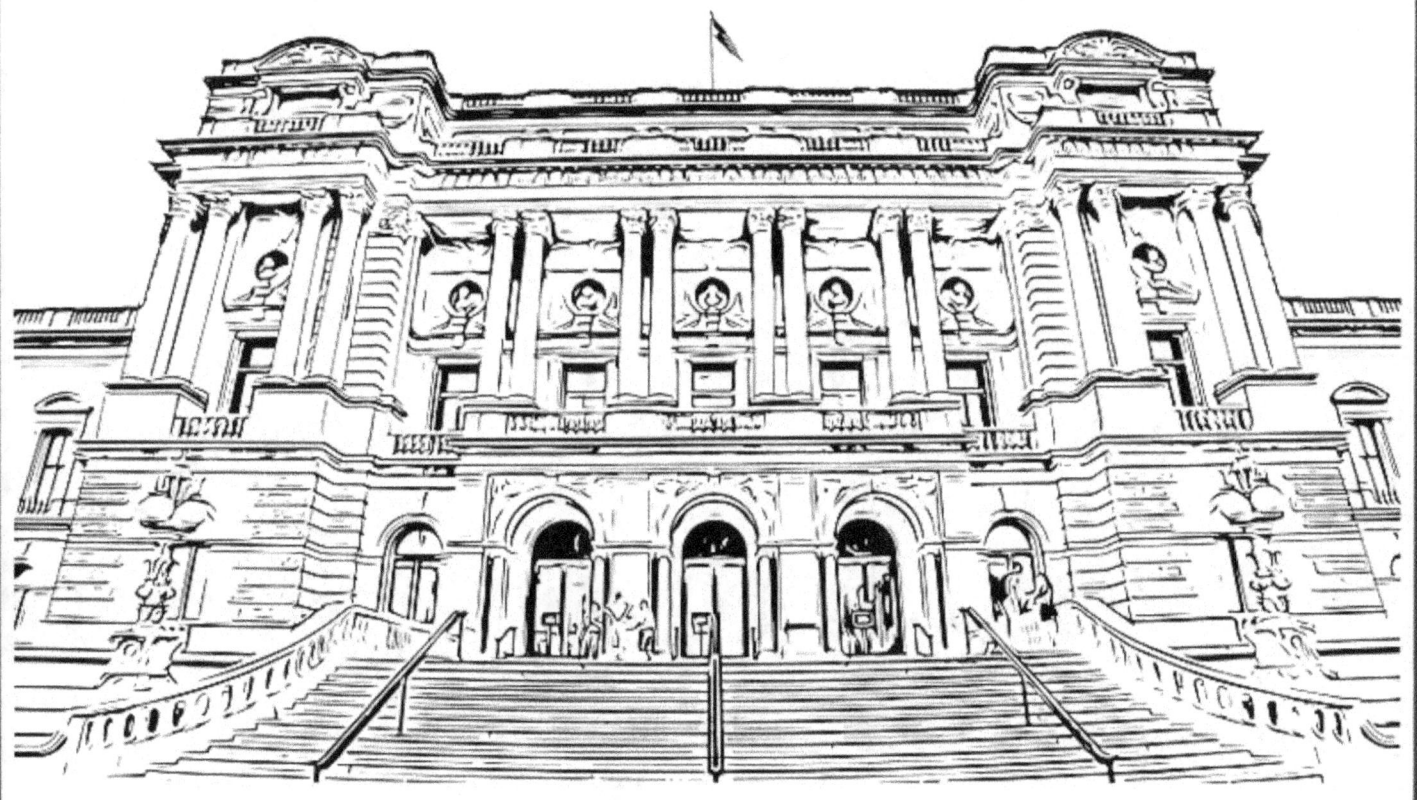

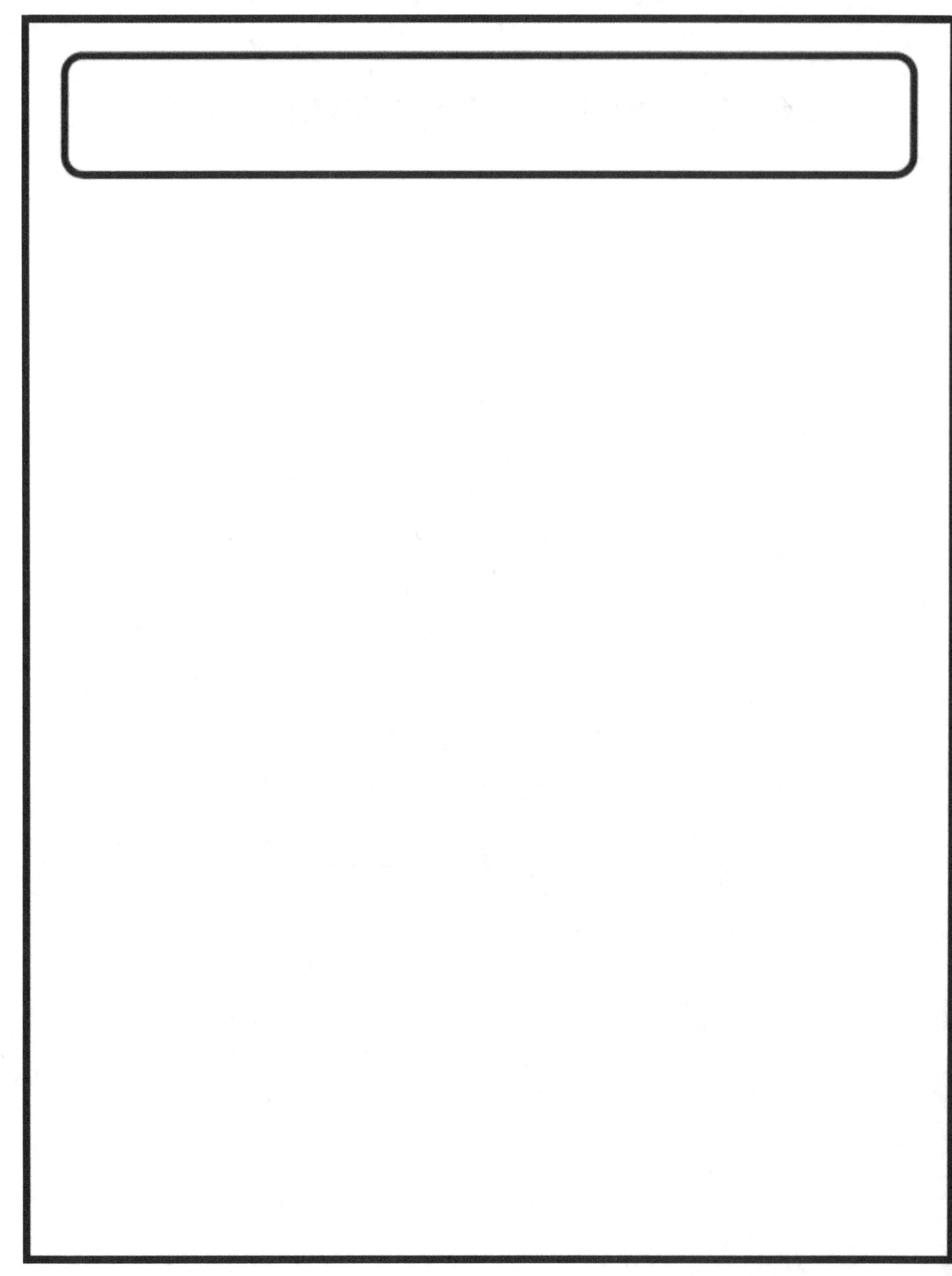

SKYSCRAPERS COLORING BOOK

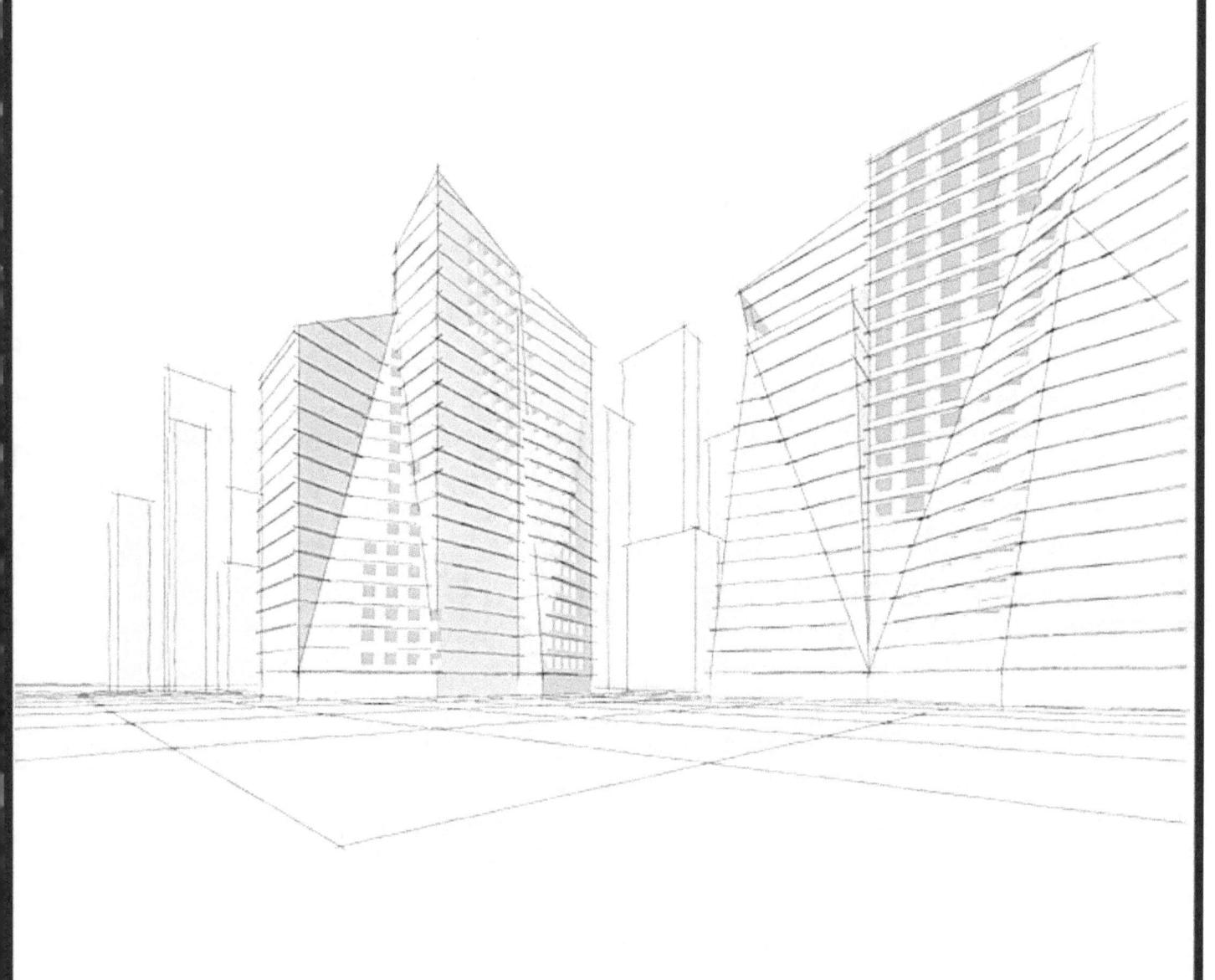

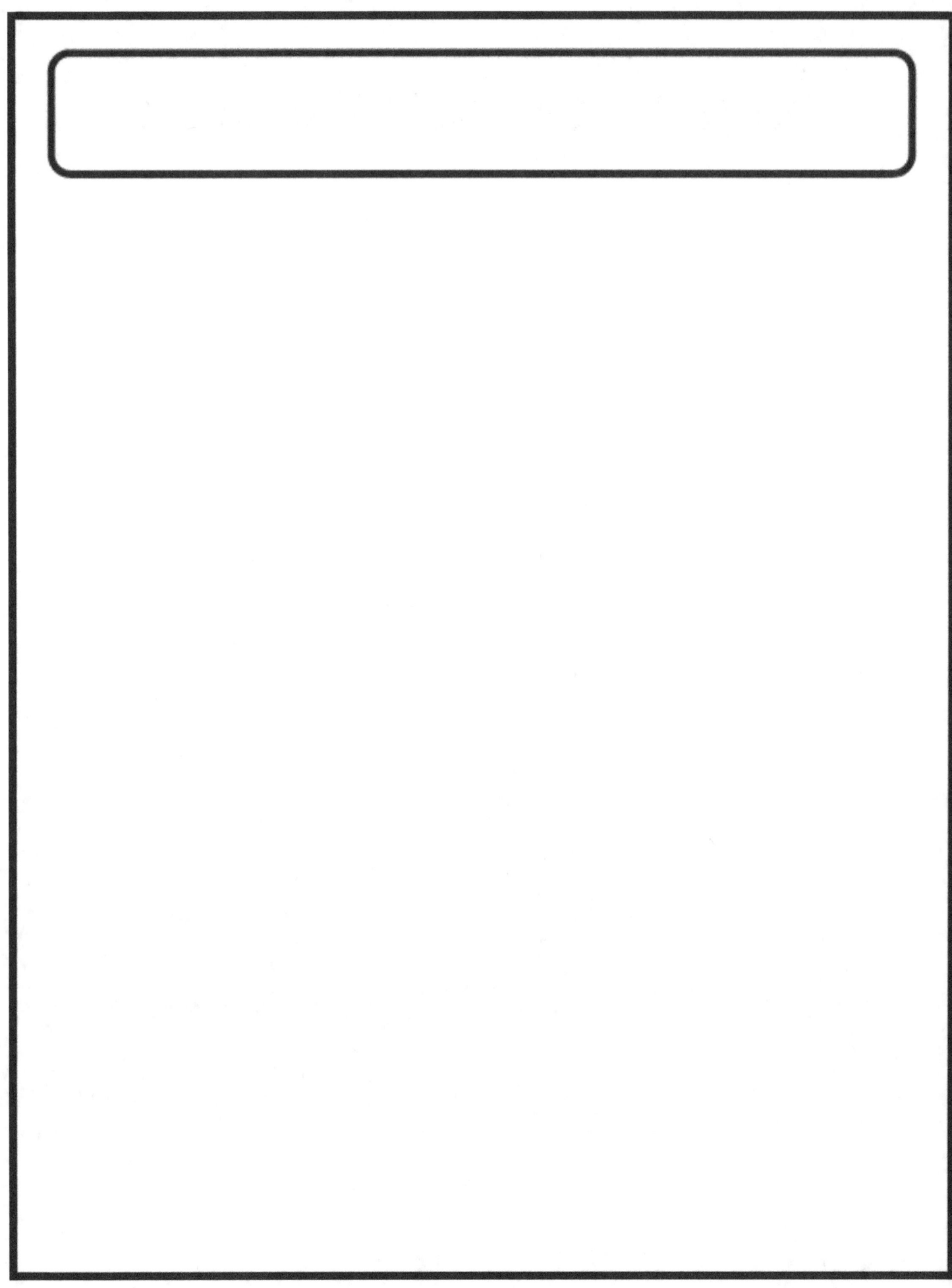

SKYSCRAPERS COLORING BOOK

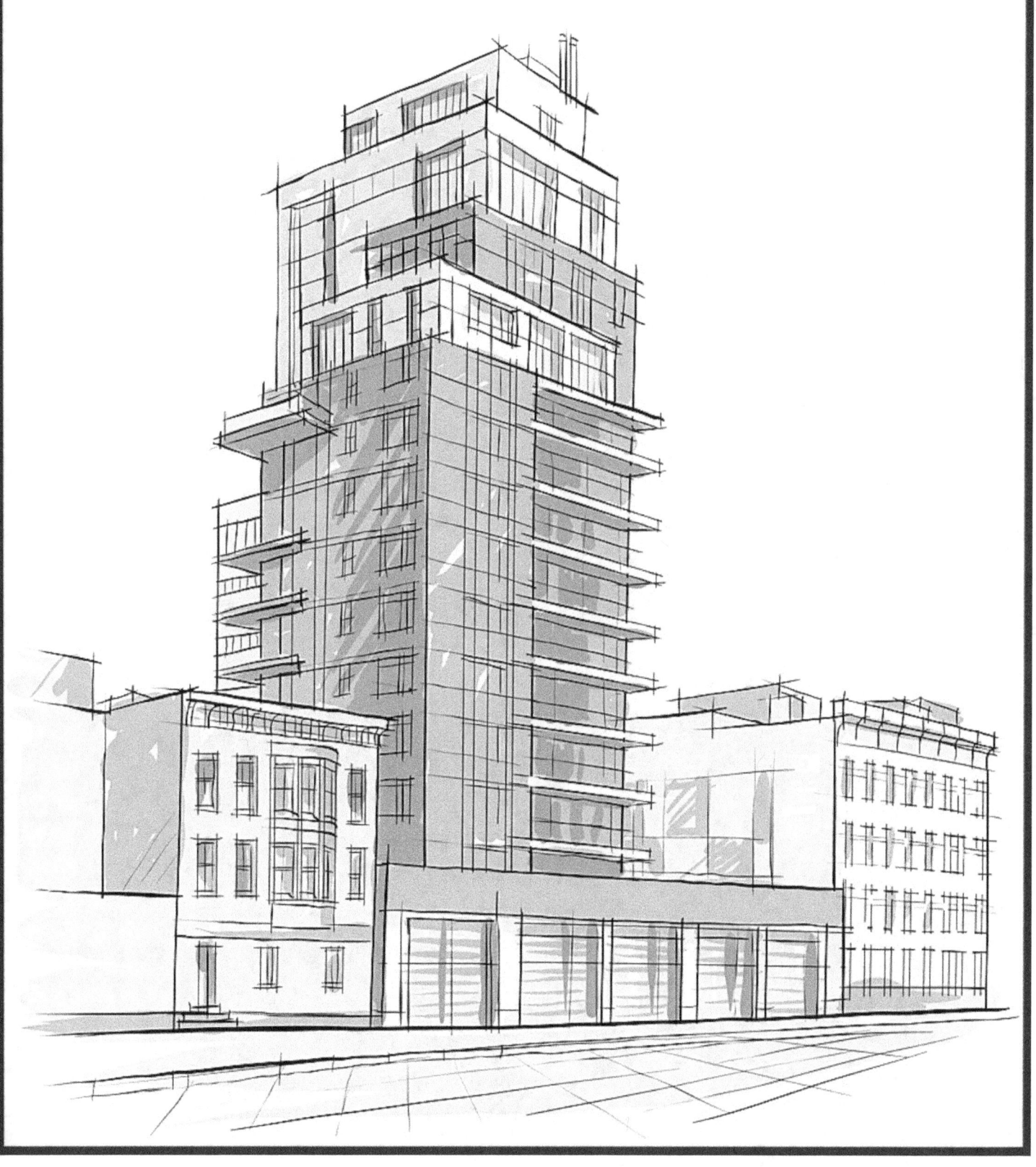

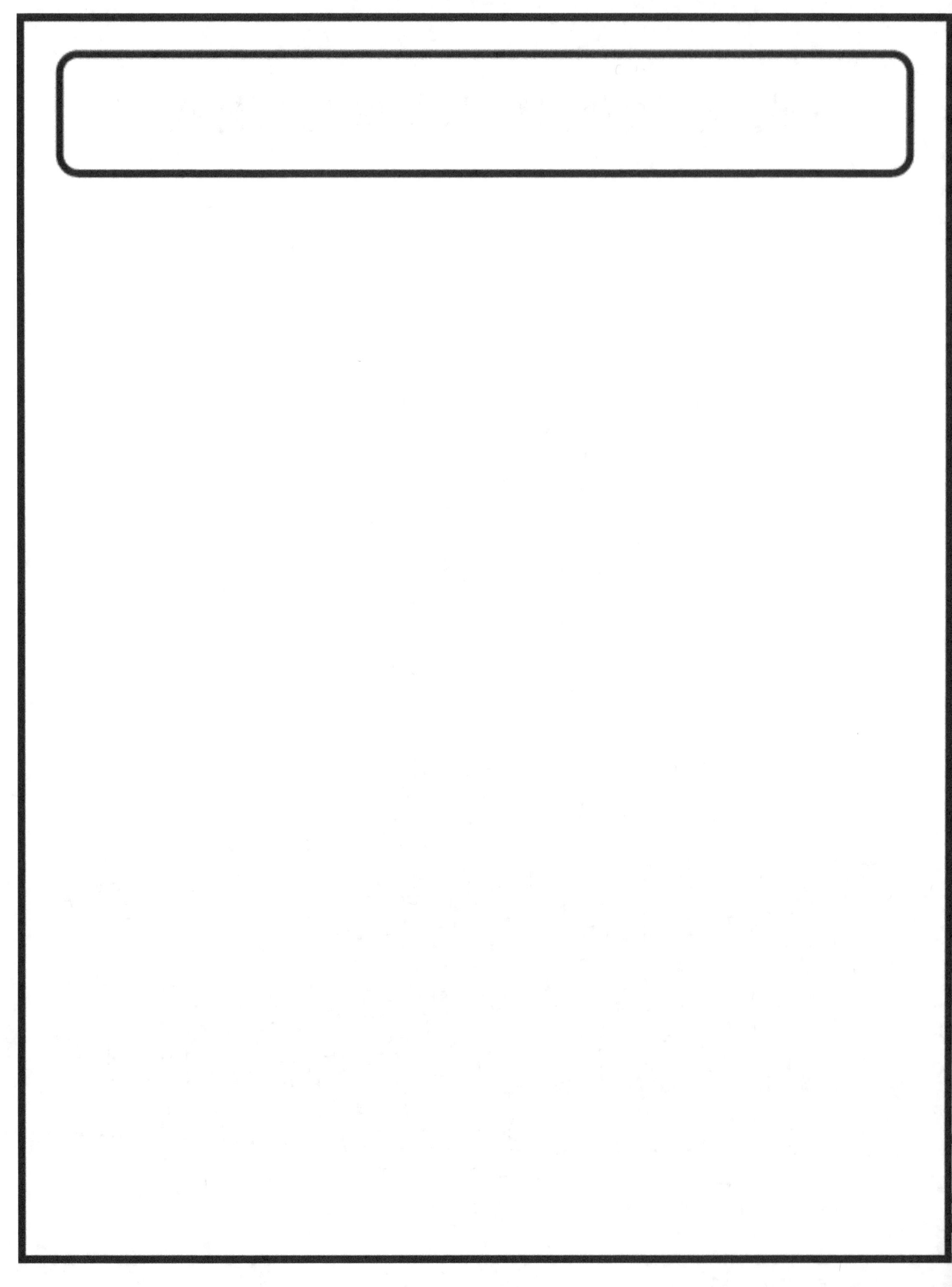

SKYSCRAPERS COLORING BOOK

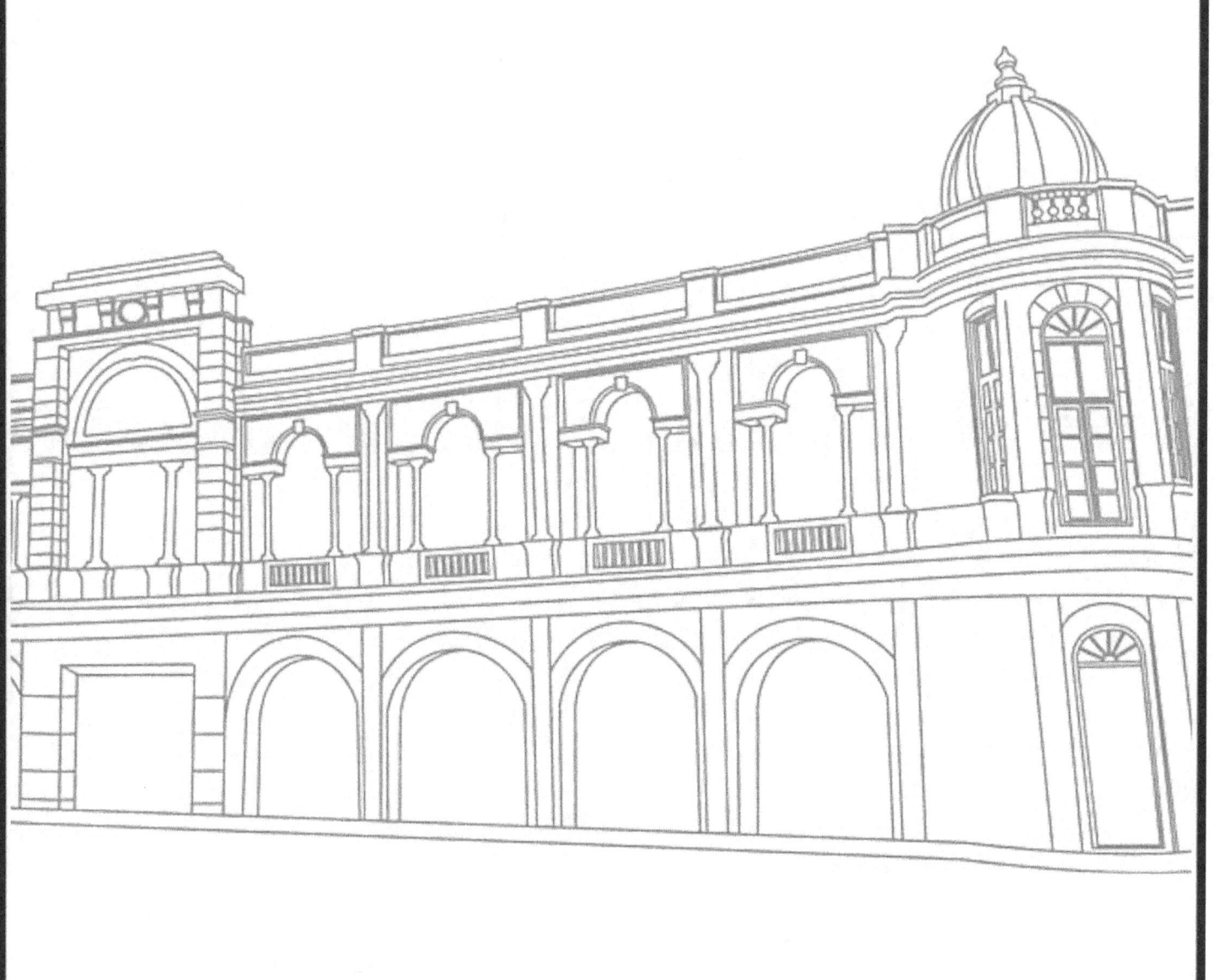

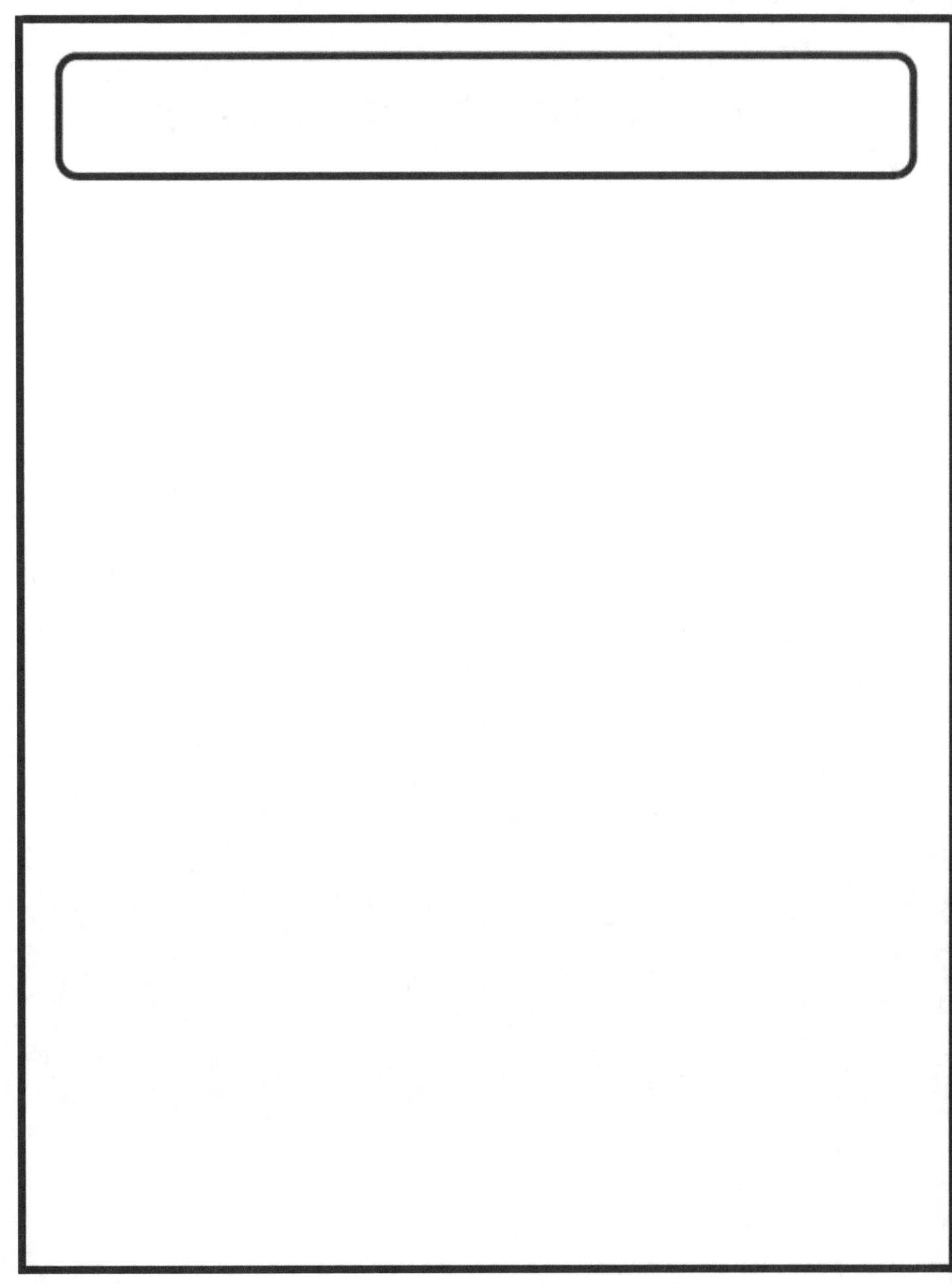

SKYSCRAPERS COLORING BOOK

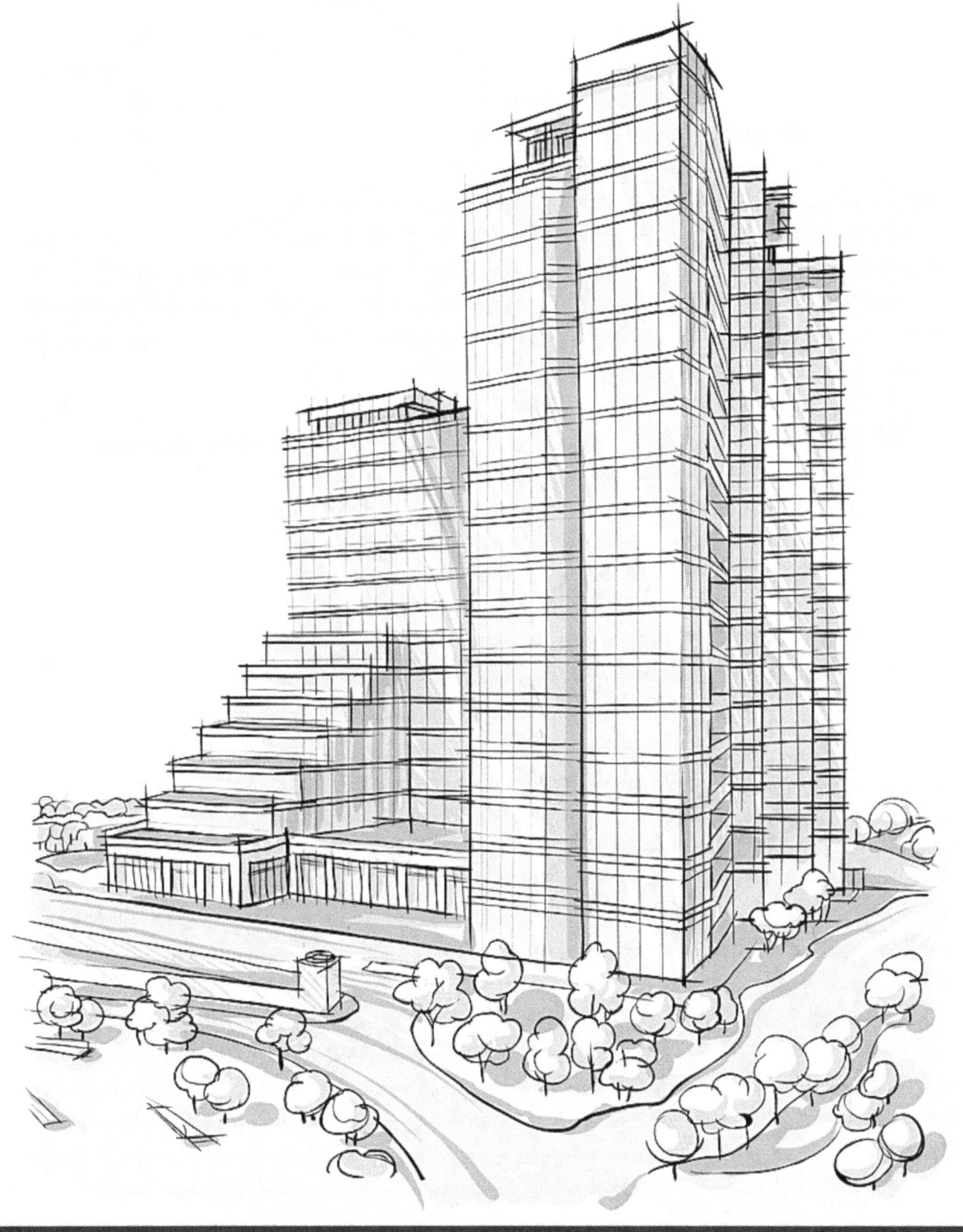

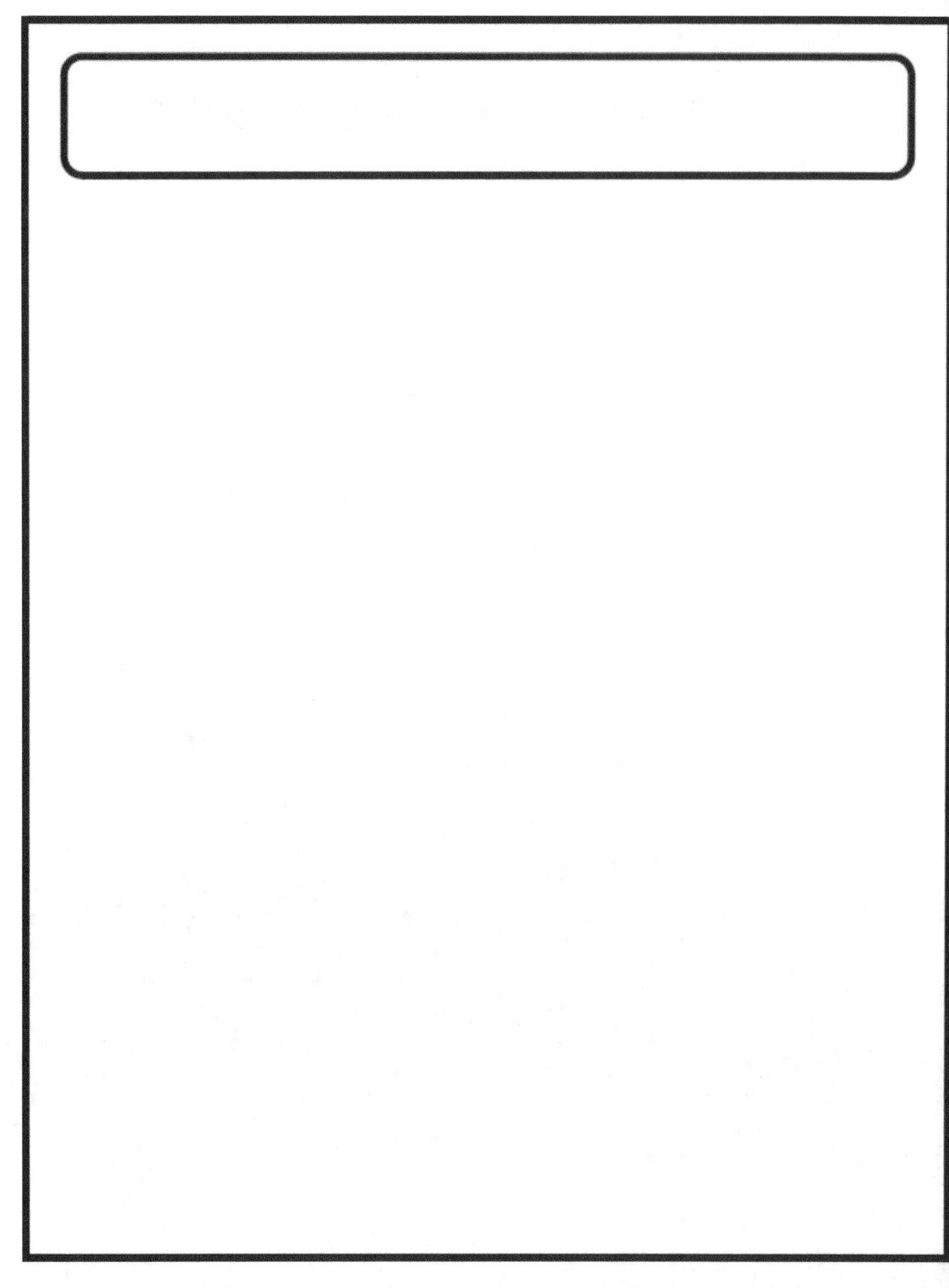

SKYSCRAPERS COLORING BOOK

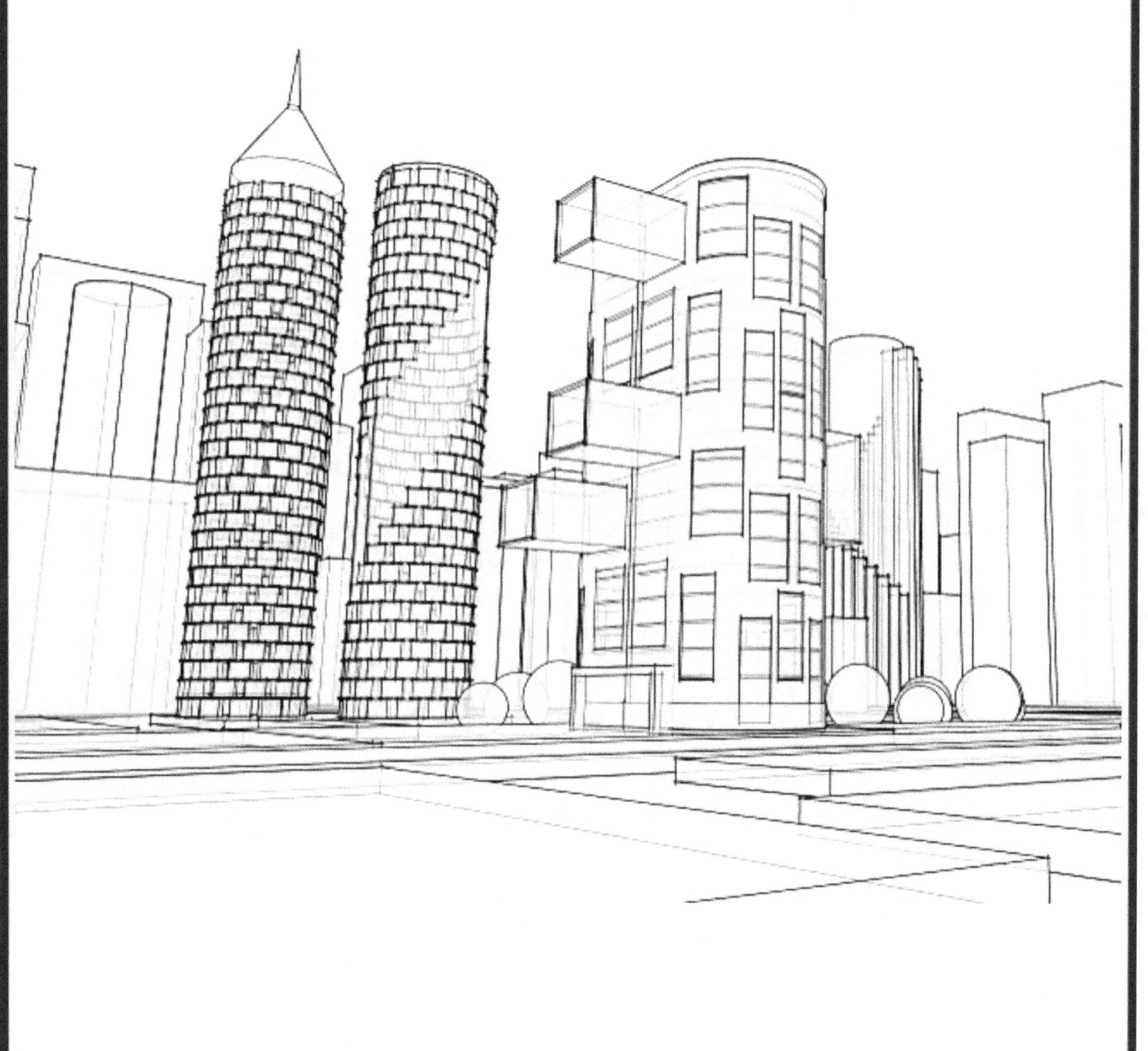

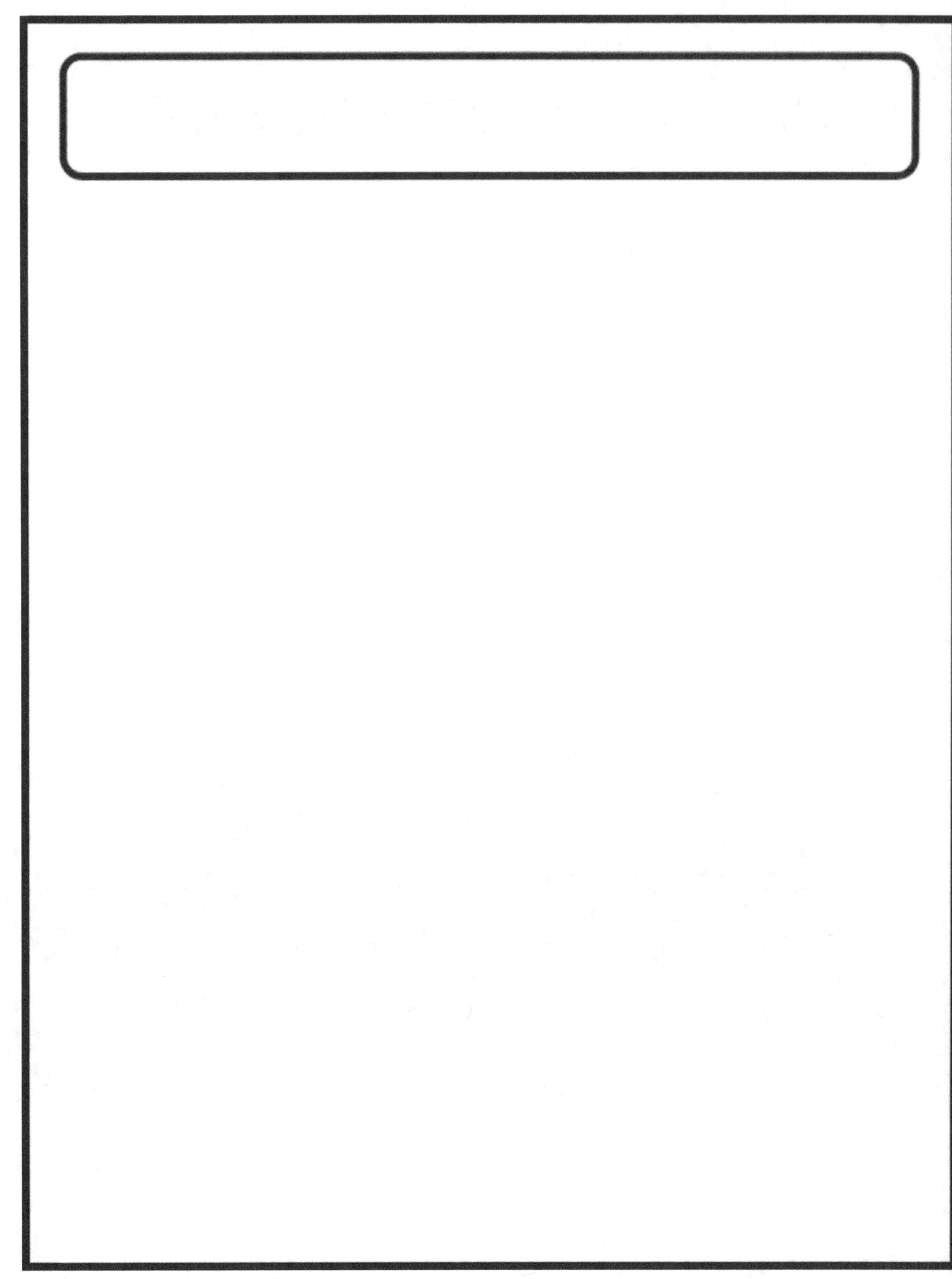

SKYSCRAPERS COLORING BOOK

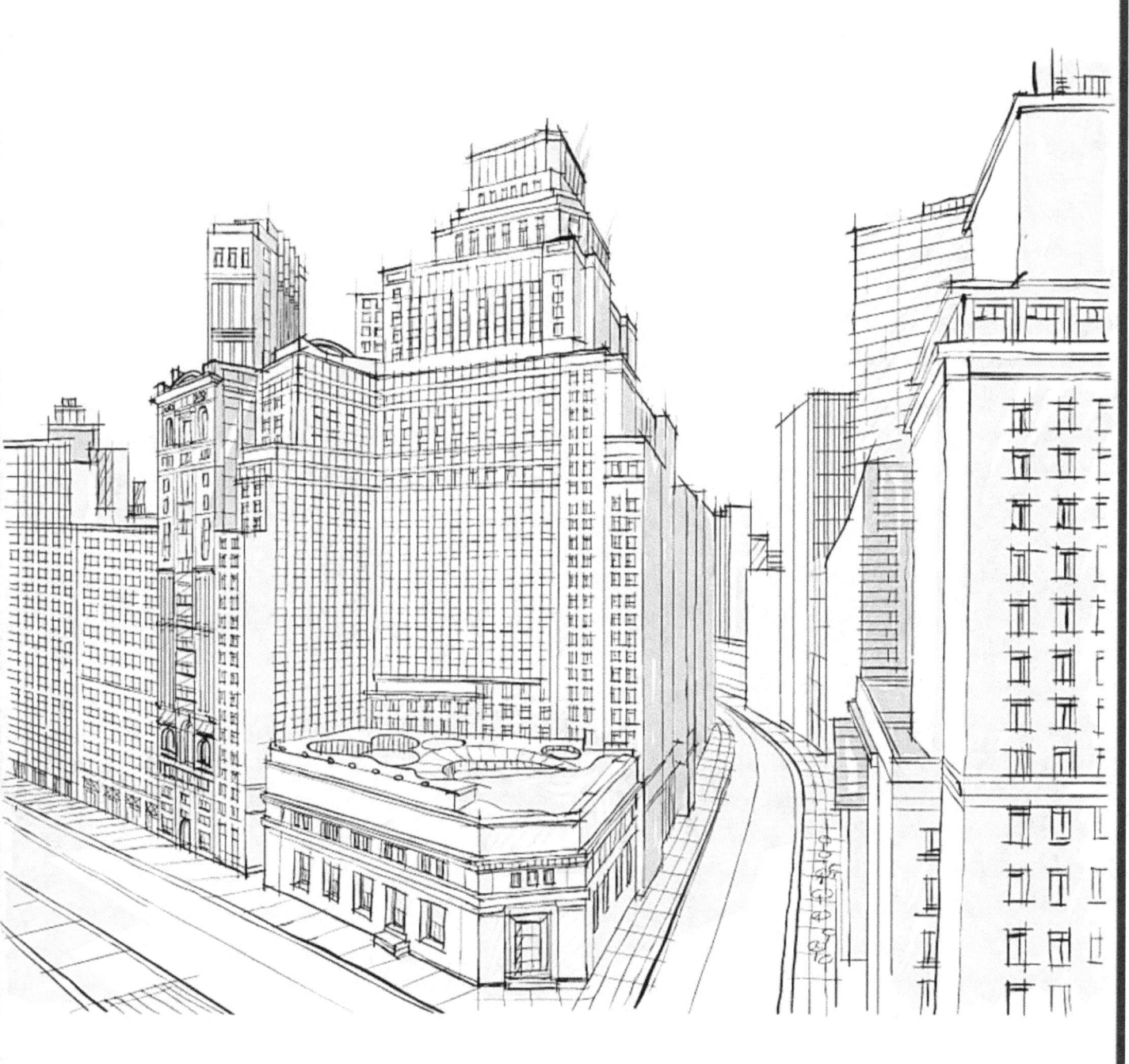

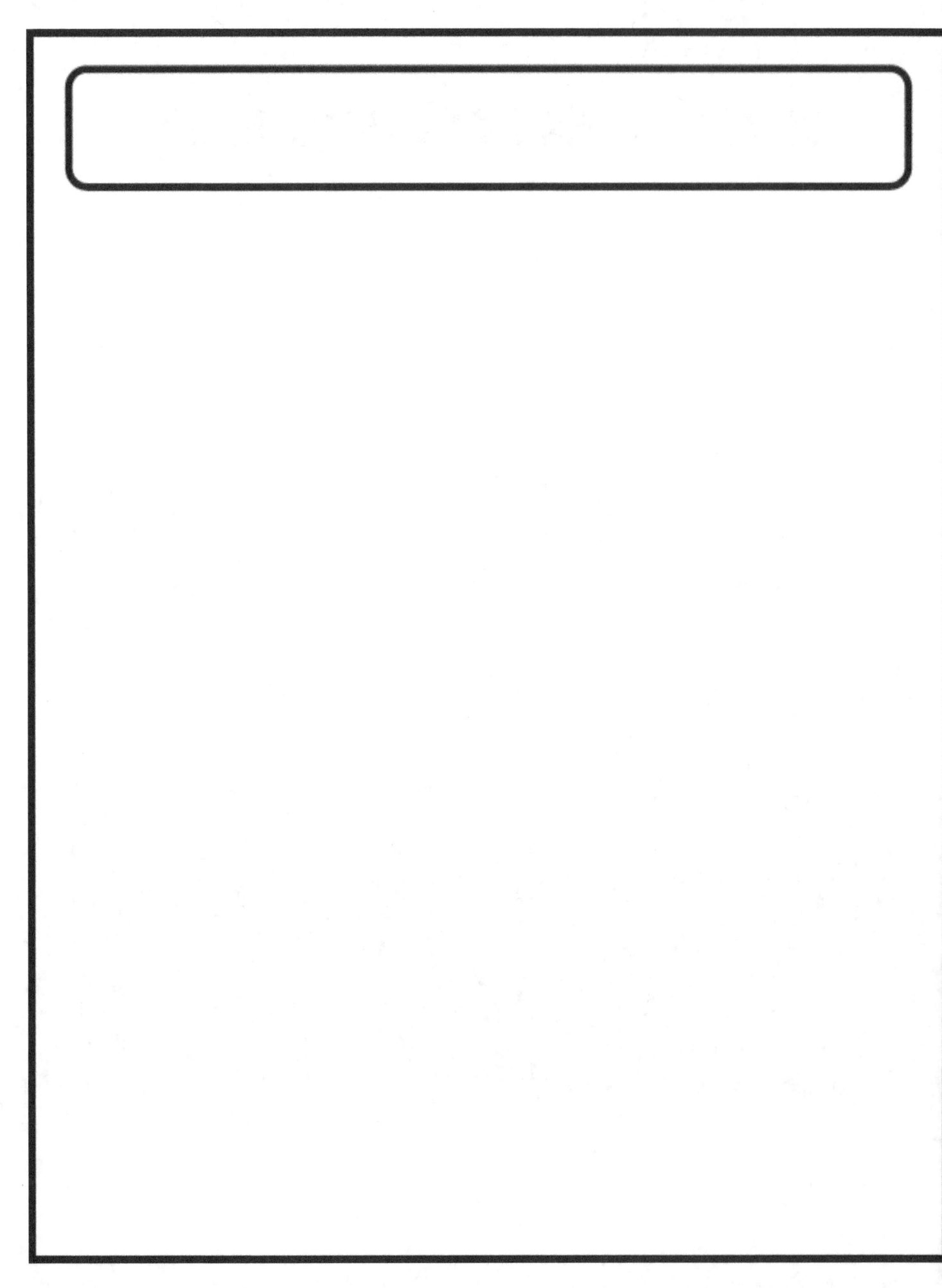

SKYSCRAPERS COLORING BOOK

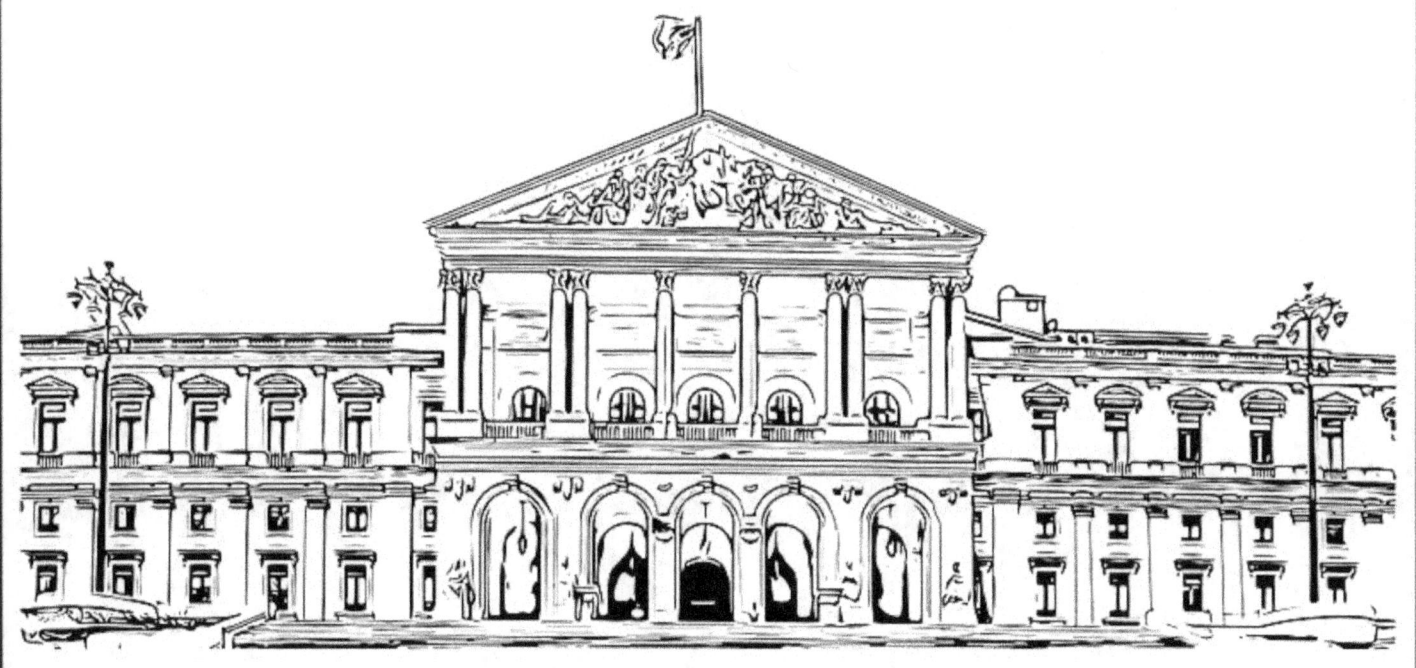

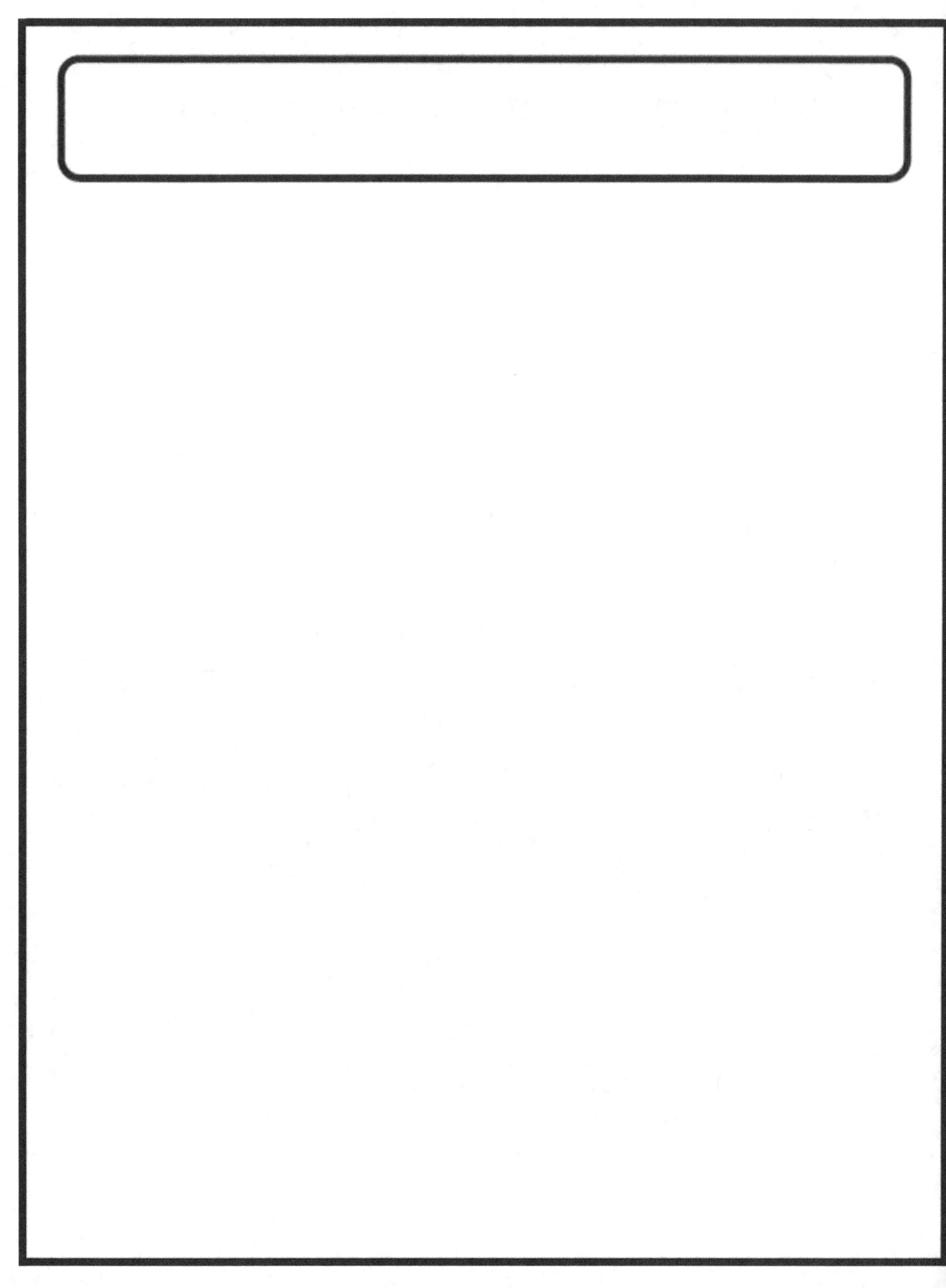

SKYSCRAPERS COLORING BOOK

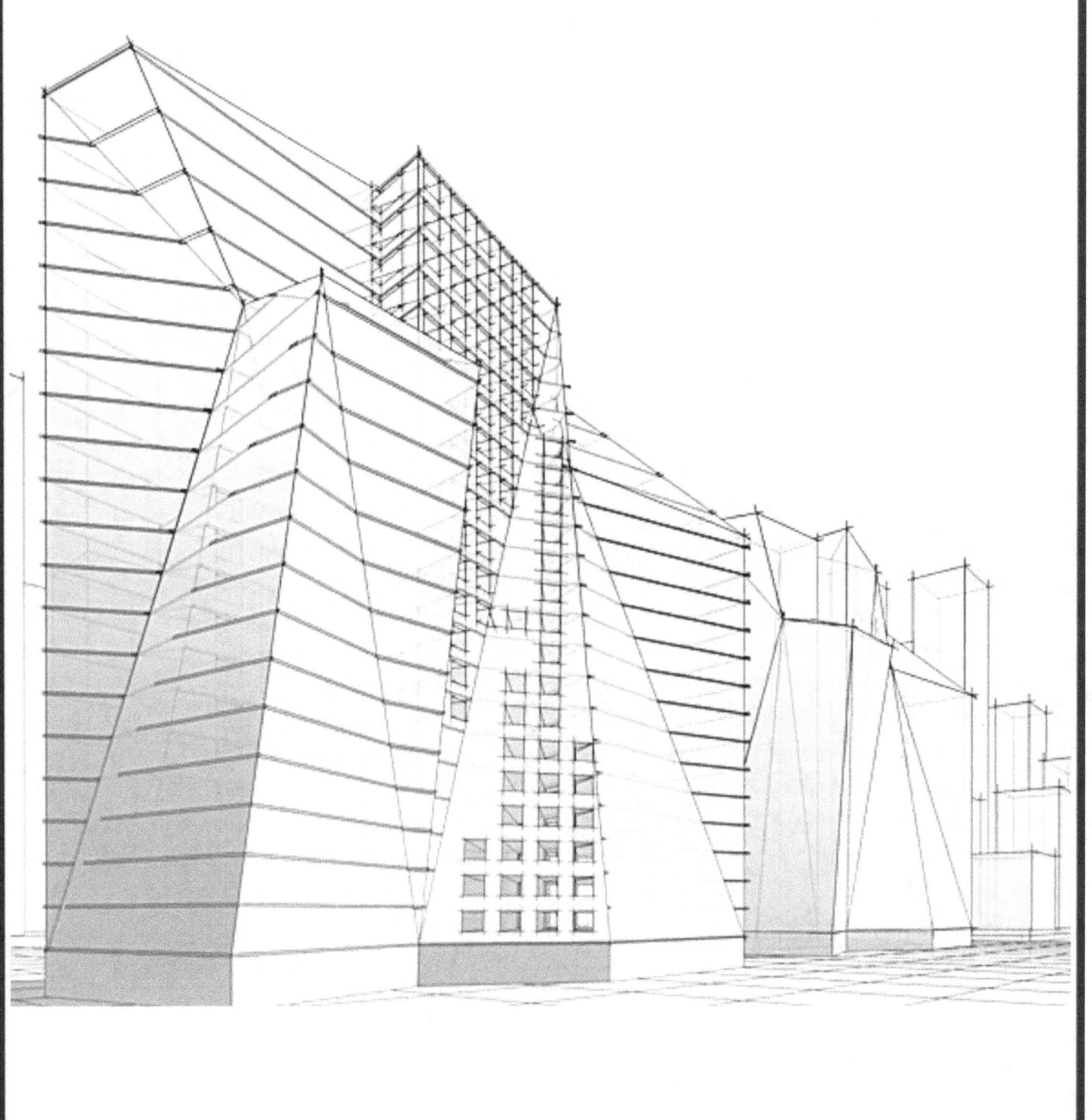

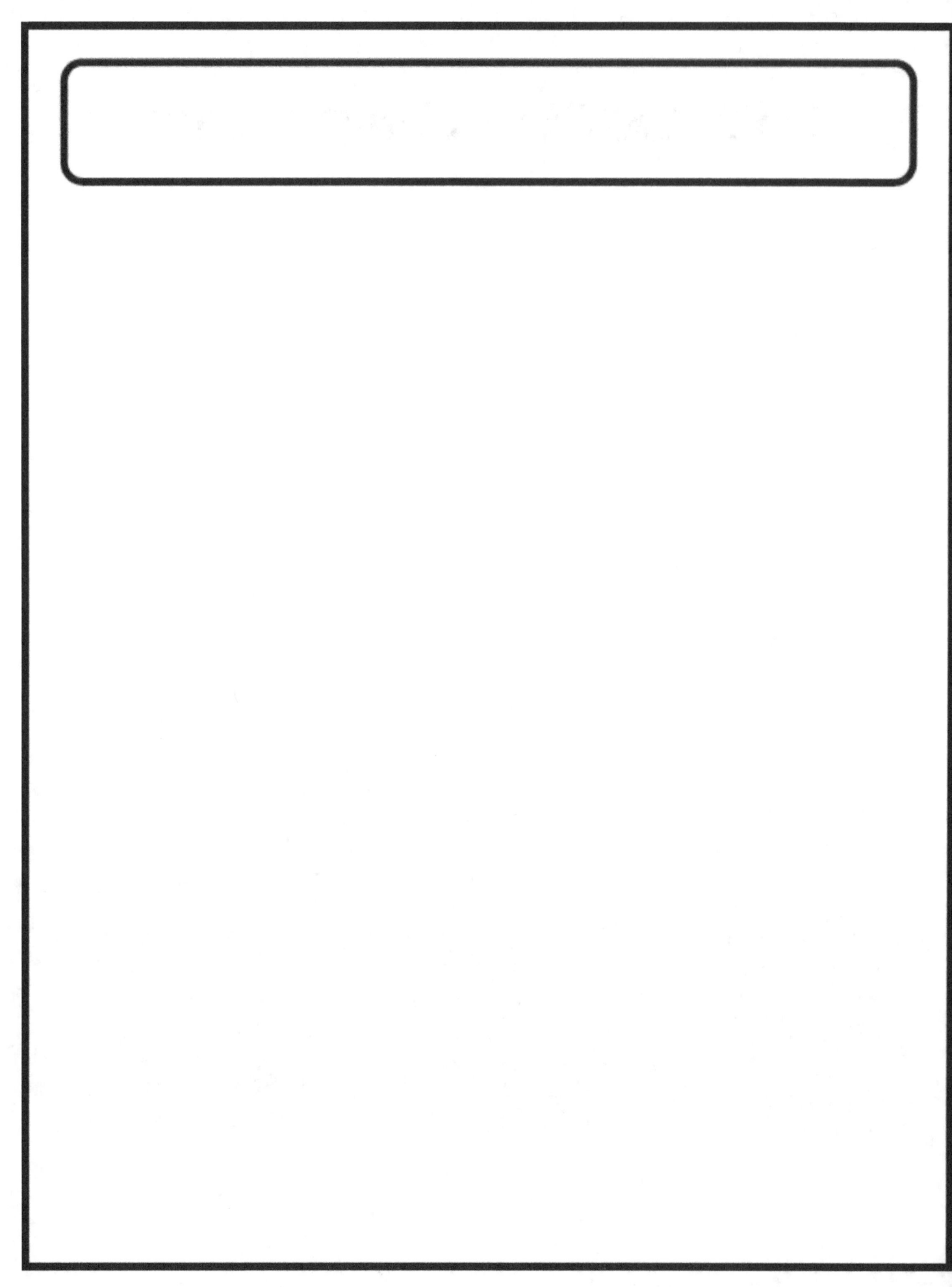

SKYSCRAPERS COLORING BOOK

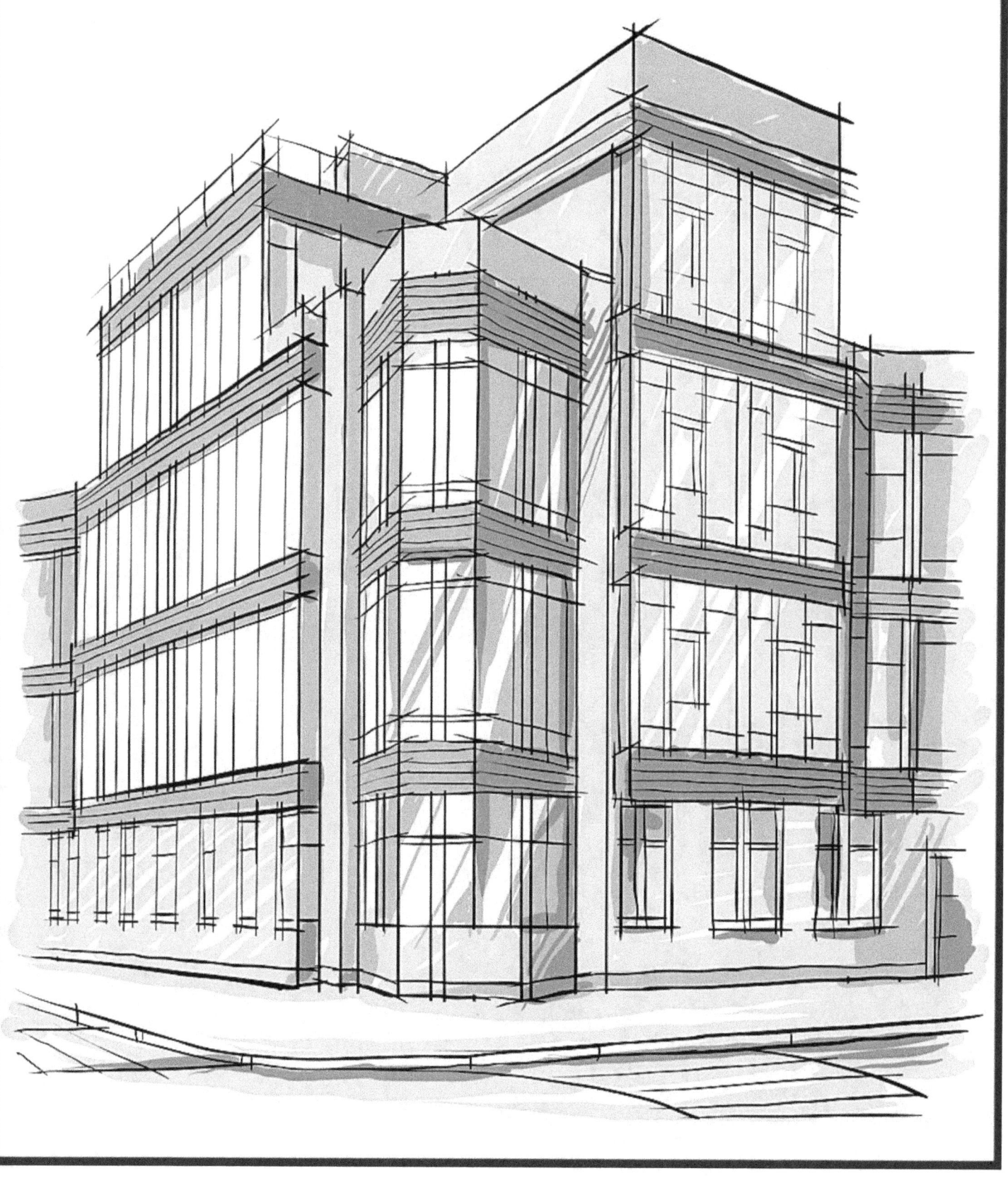

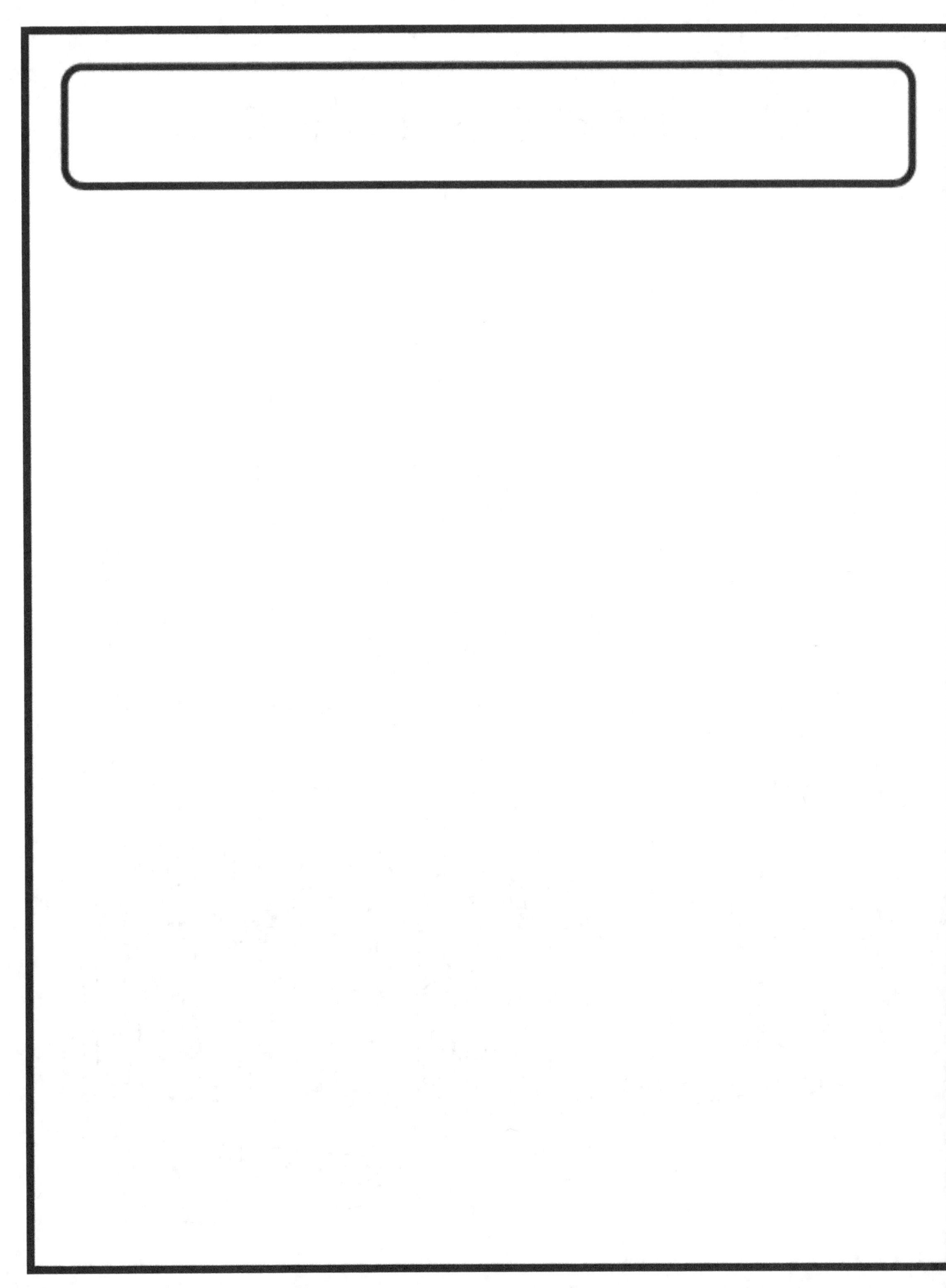

SKYSCRAPERS COLORING BOOK

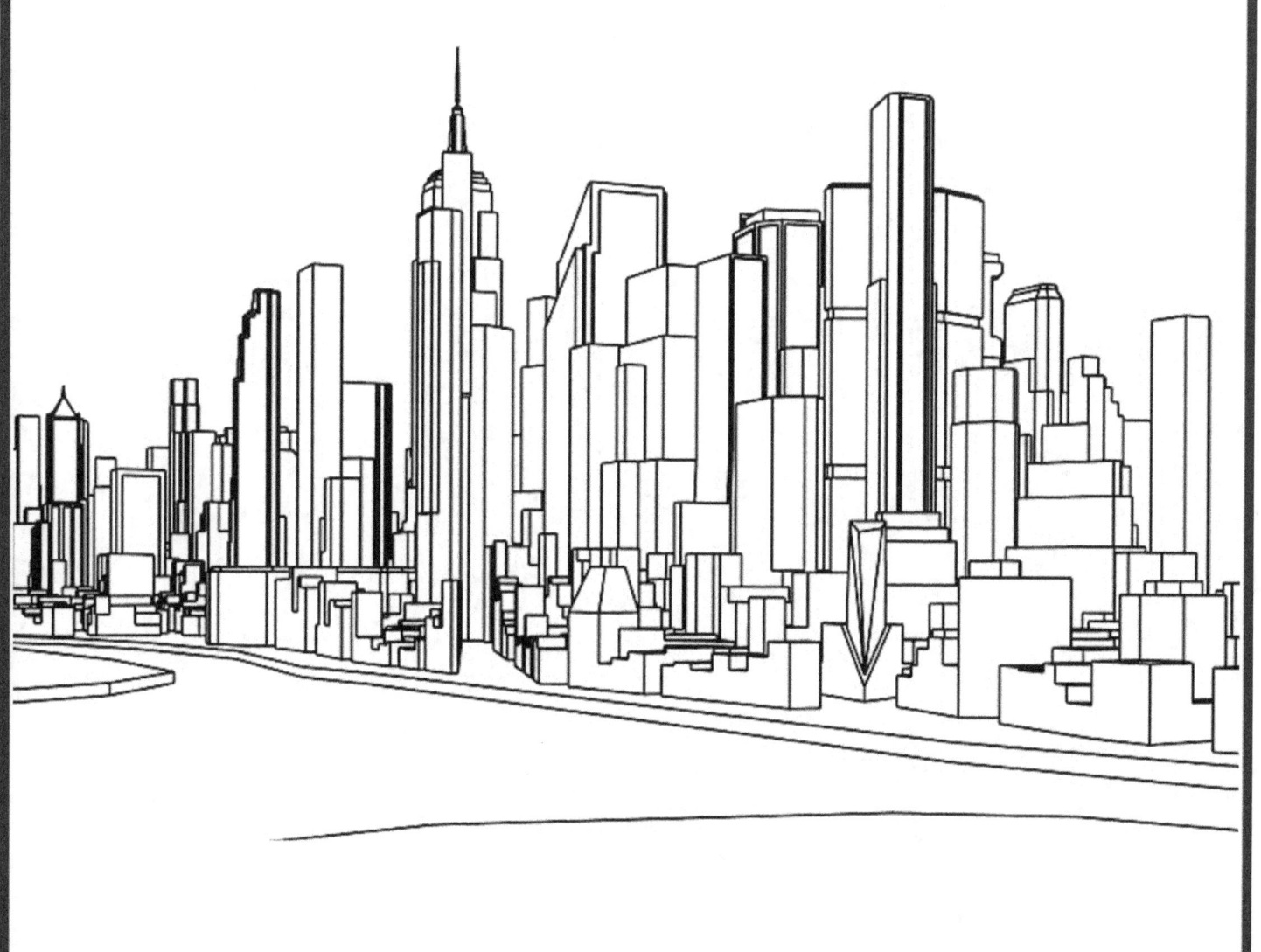

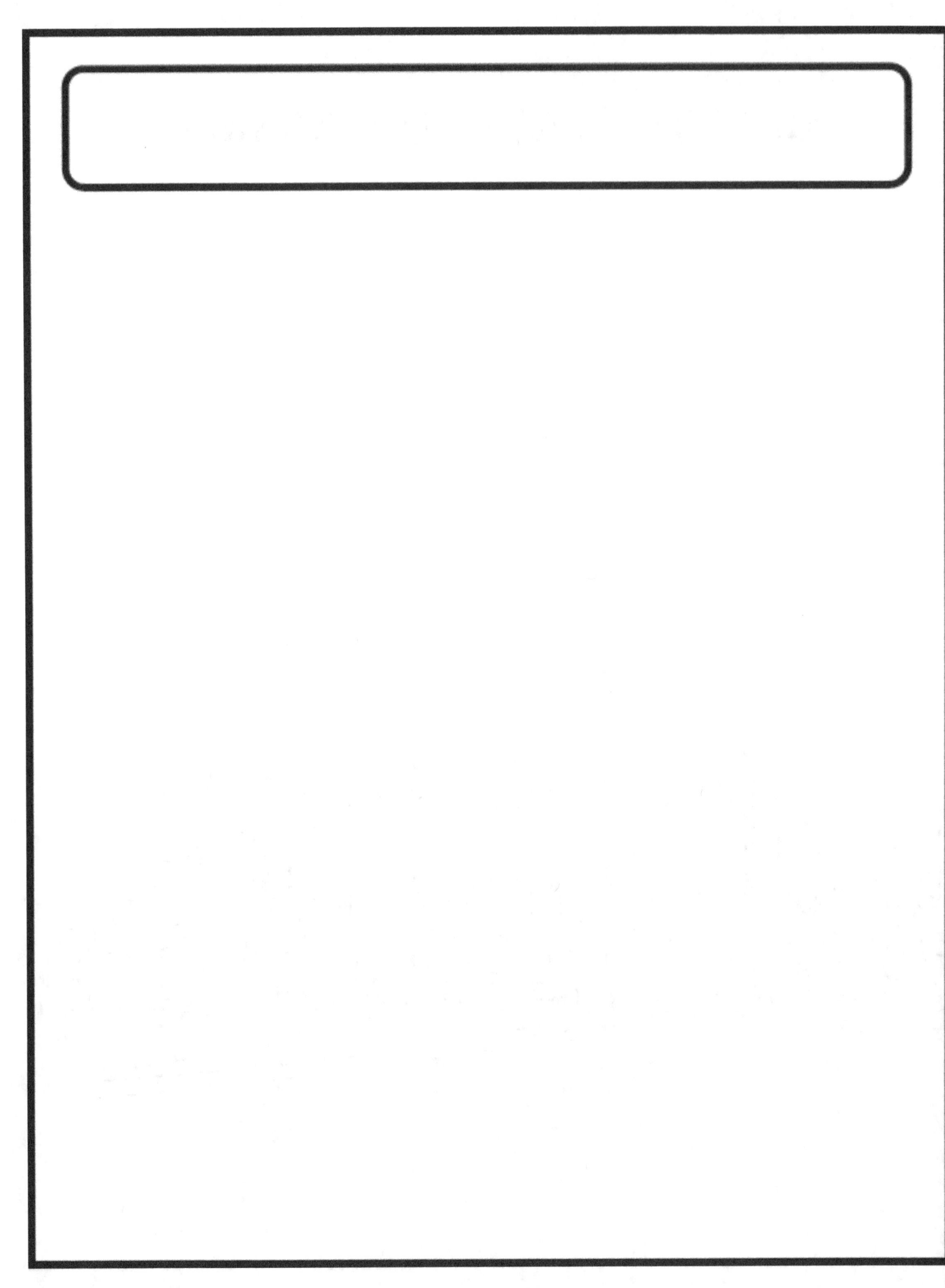

SKYSCRAPERS COLORING BOOK

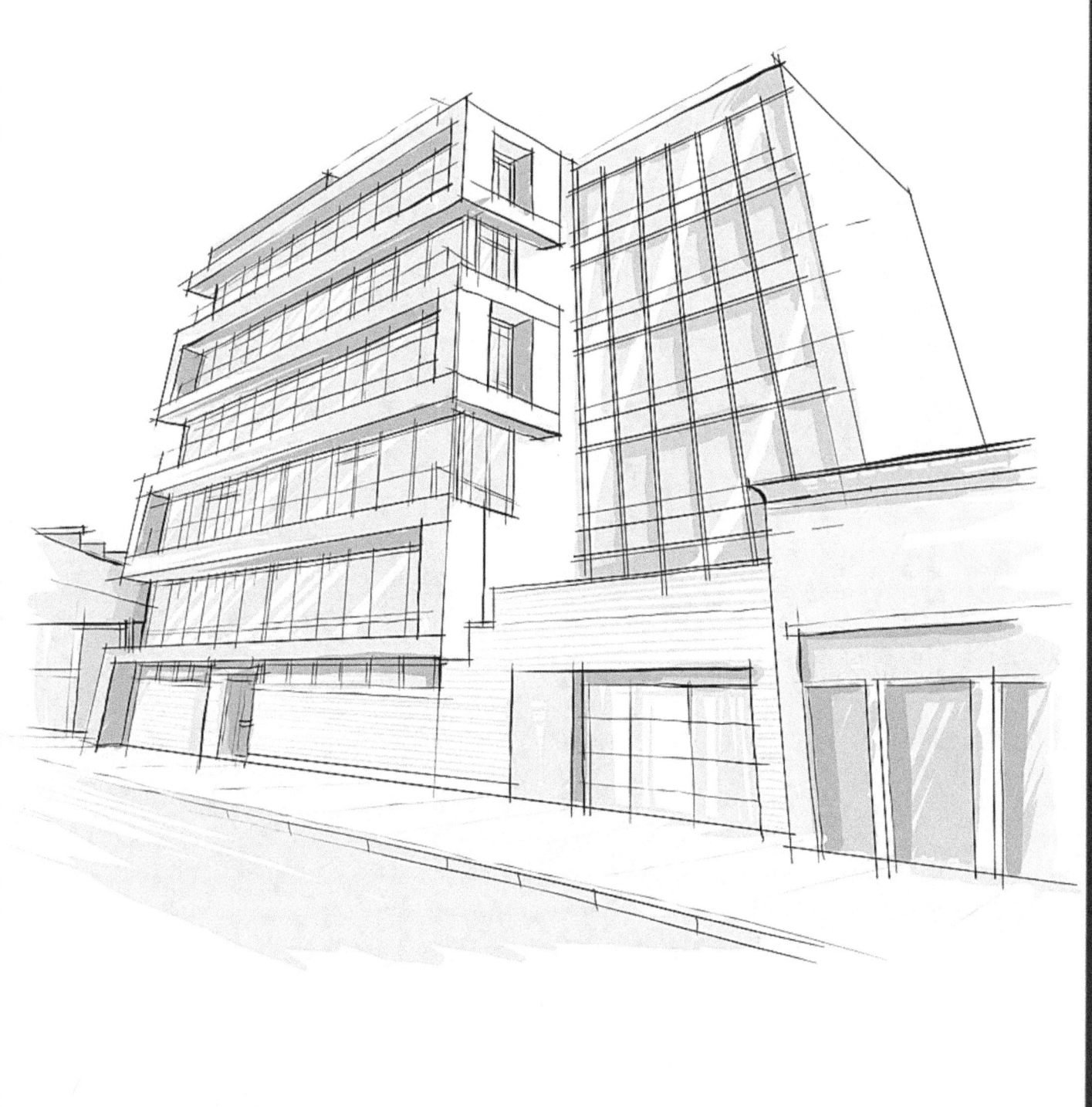

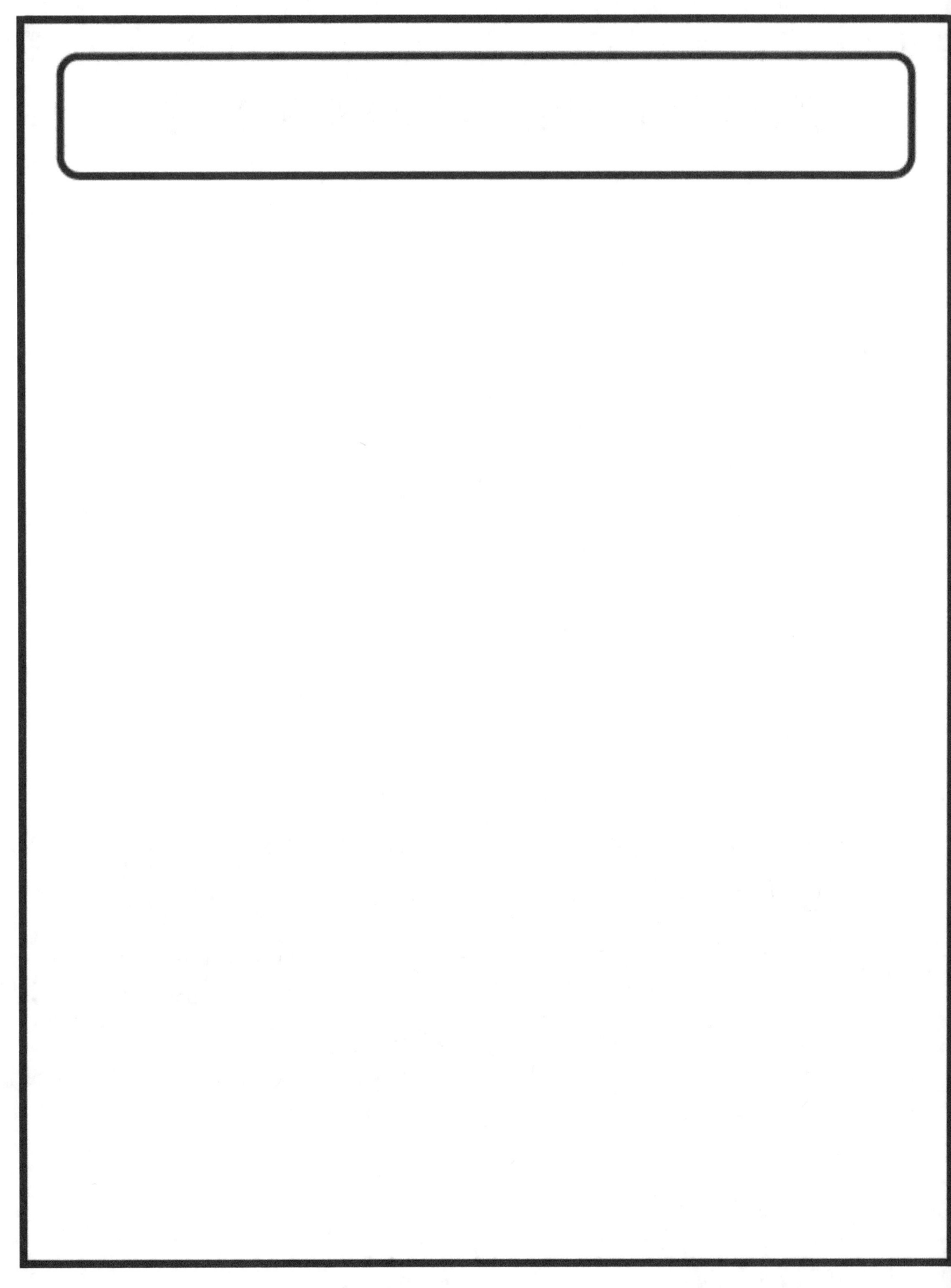

SKYSCRAPERS COLORING BOOK

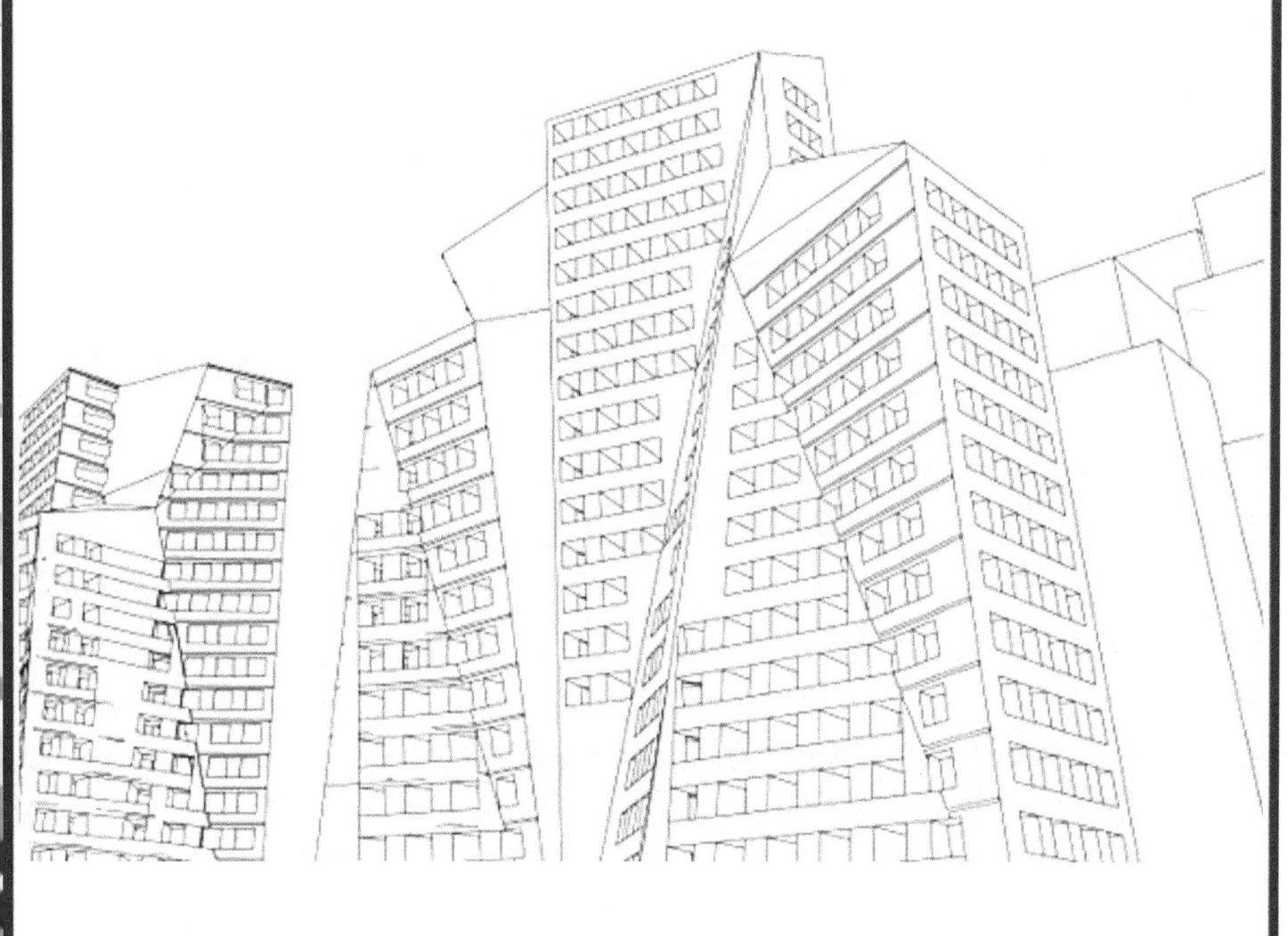

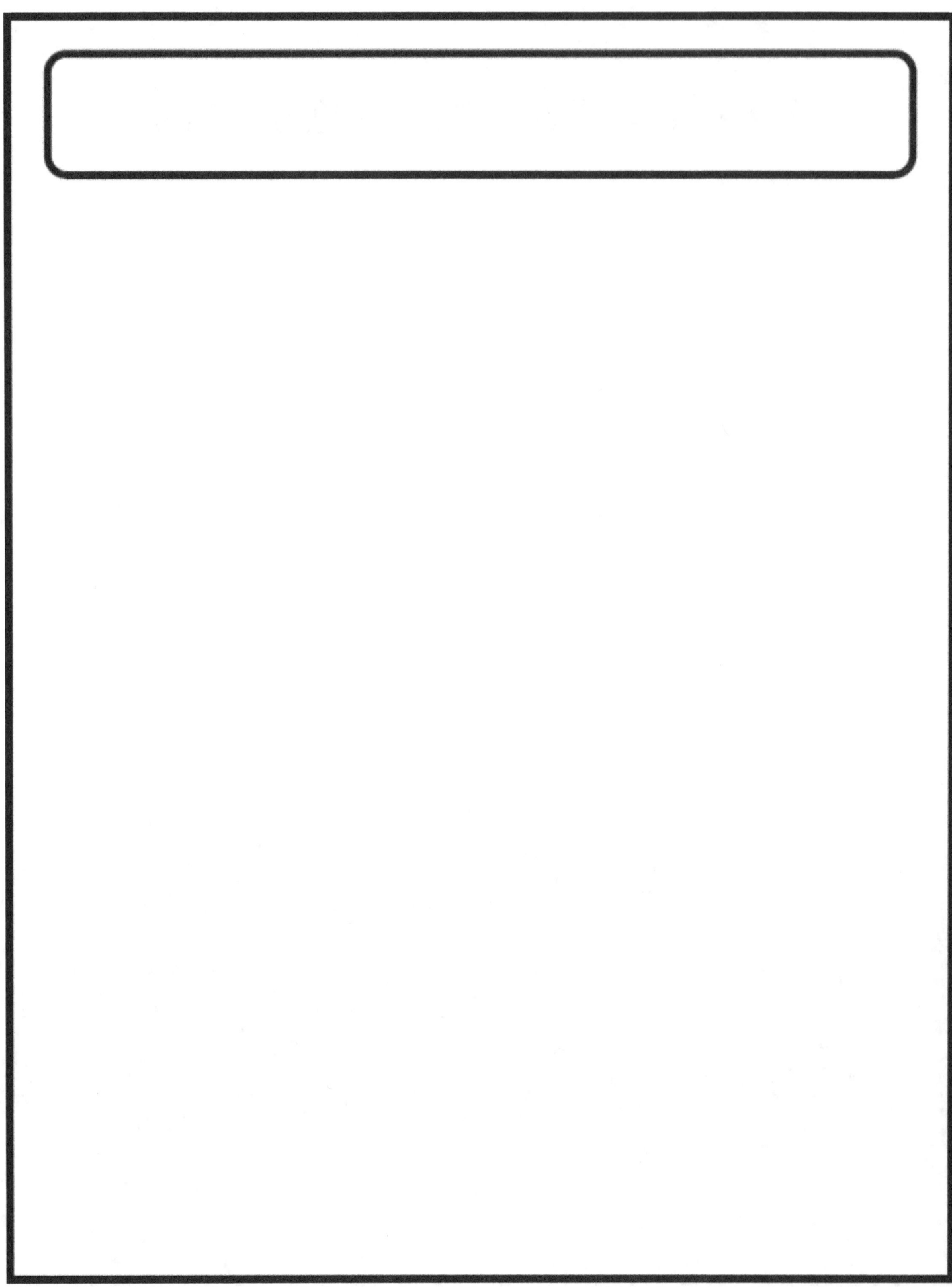

SKYSCRAPERS COLORING BOOK

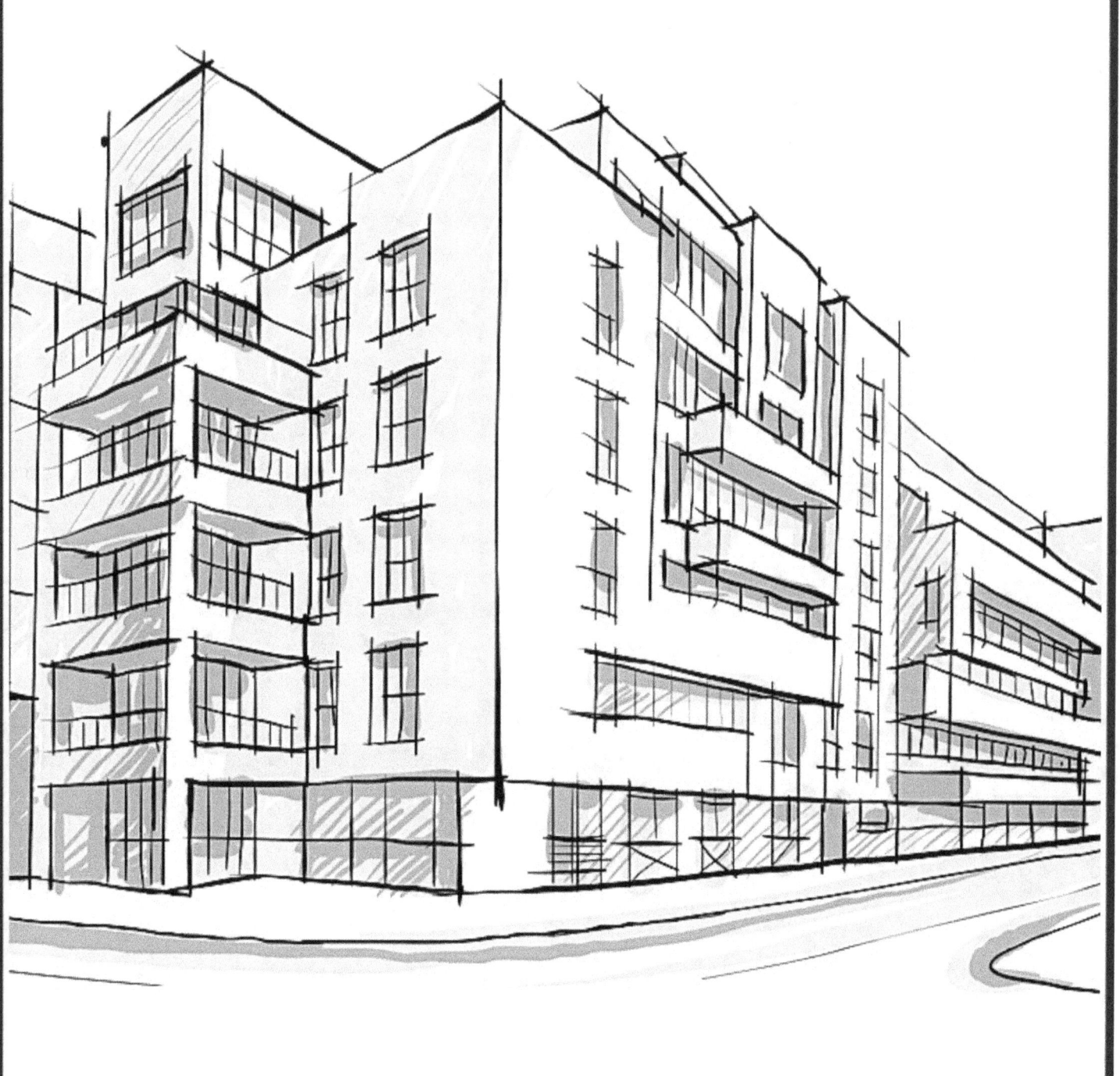

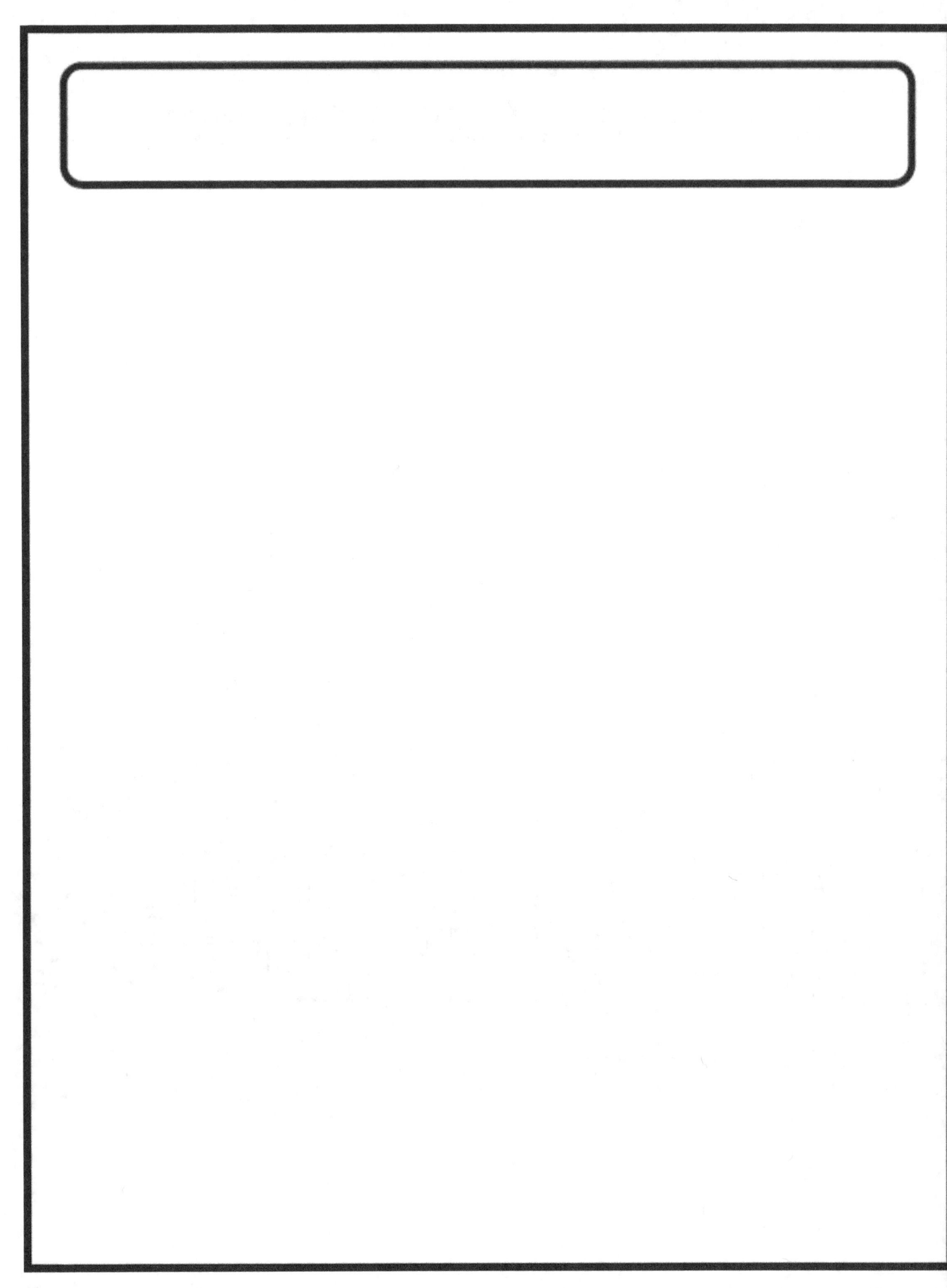

SKYSCRAPERS COLORING BOOK

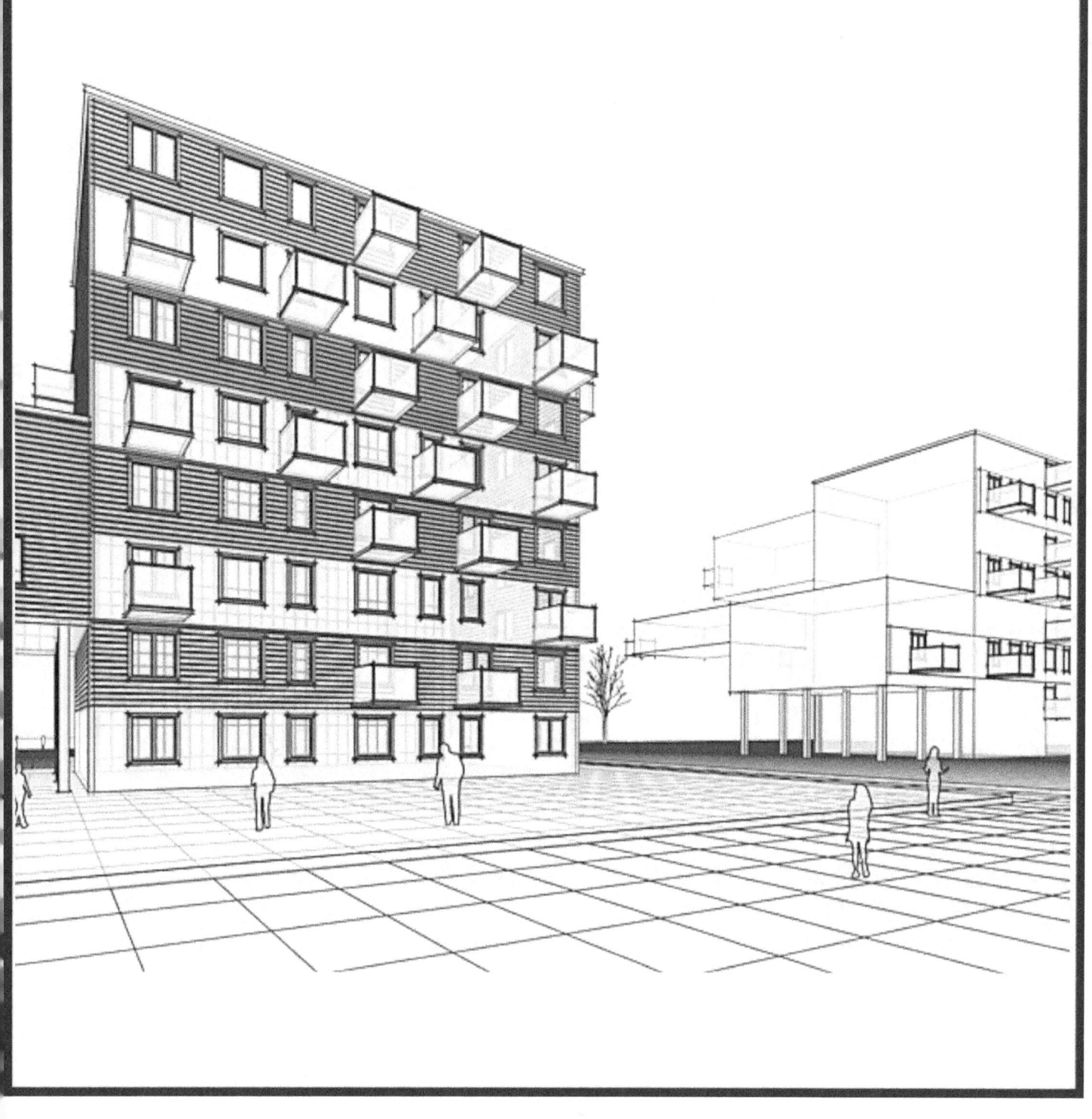

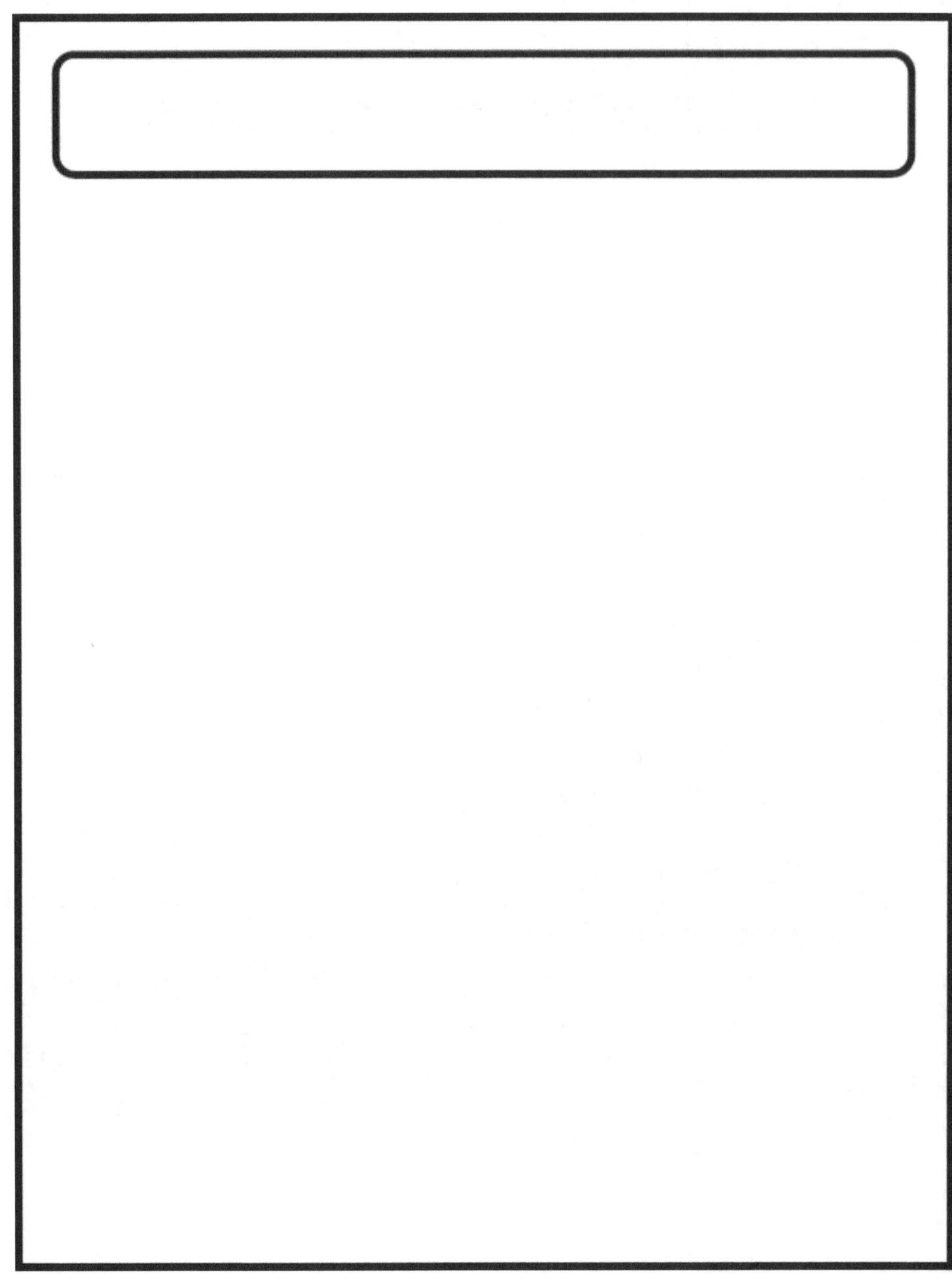

SKYSCRAPERS COLORING BOOK

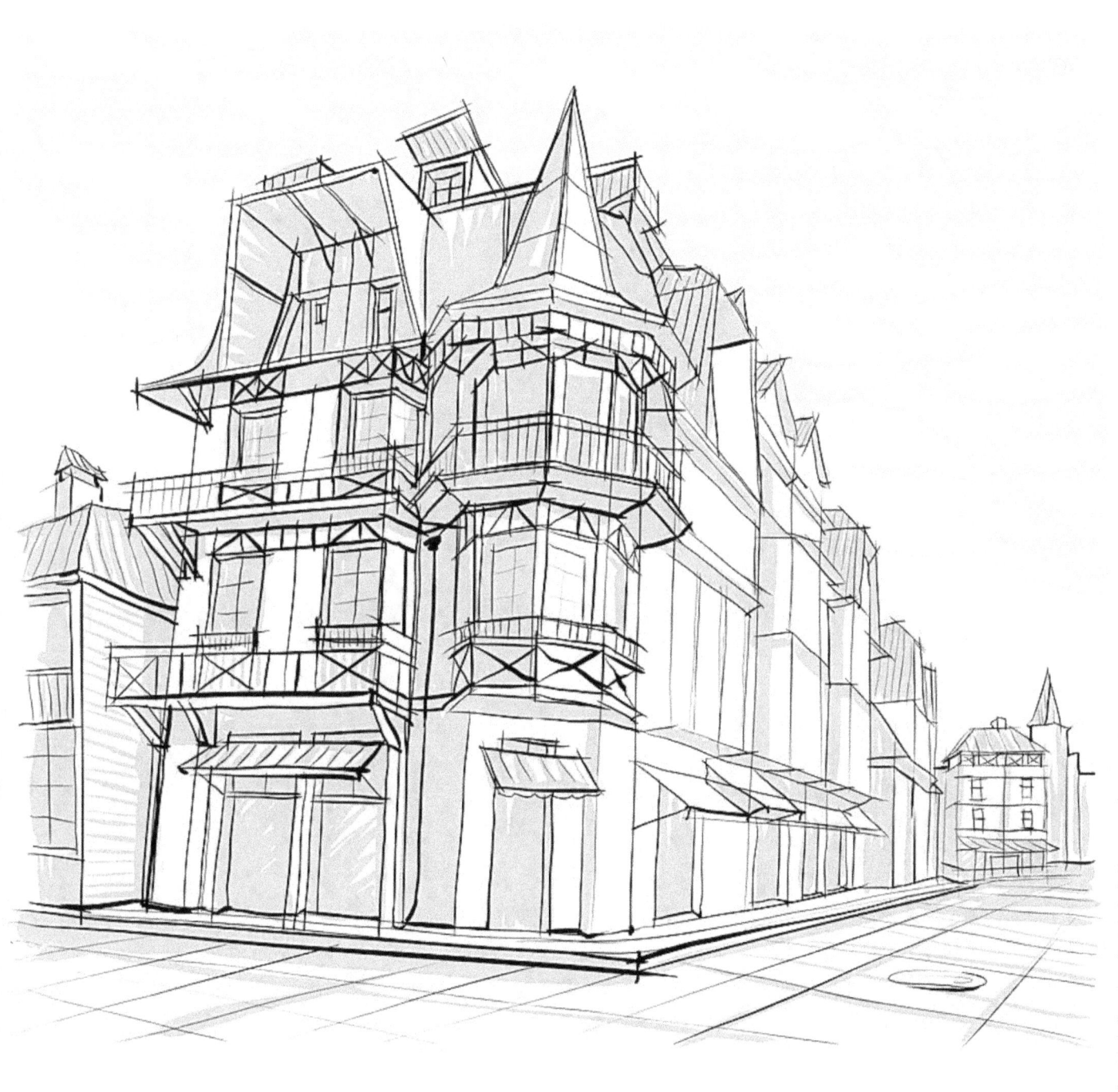

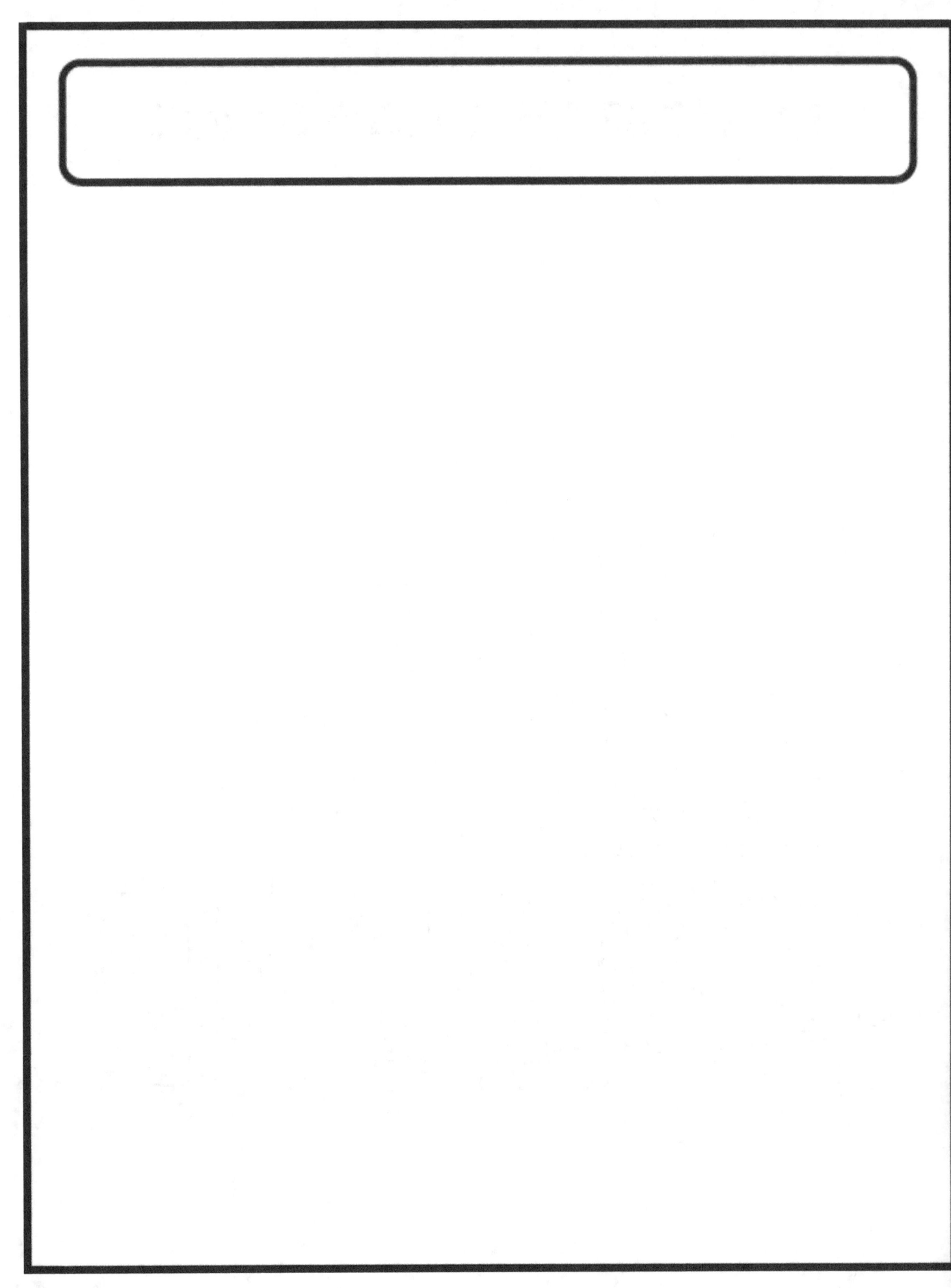

SKYSCRAPERS COLORING BOOK

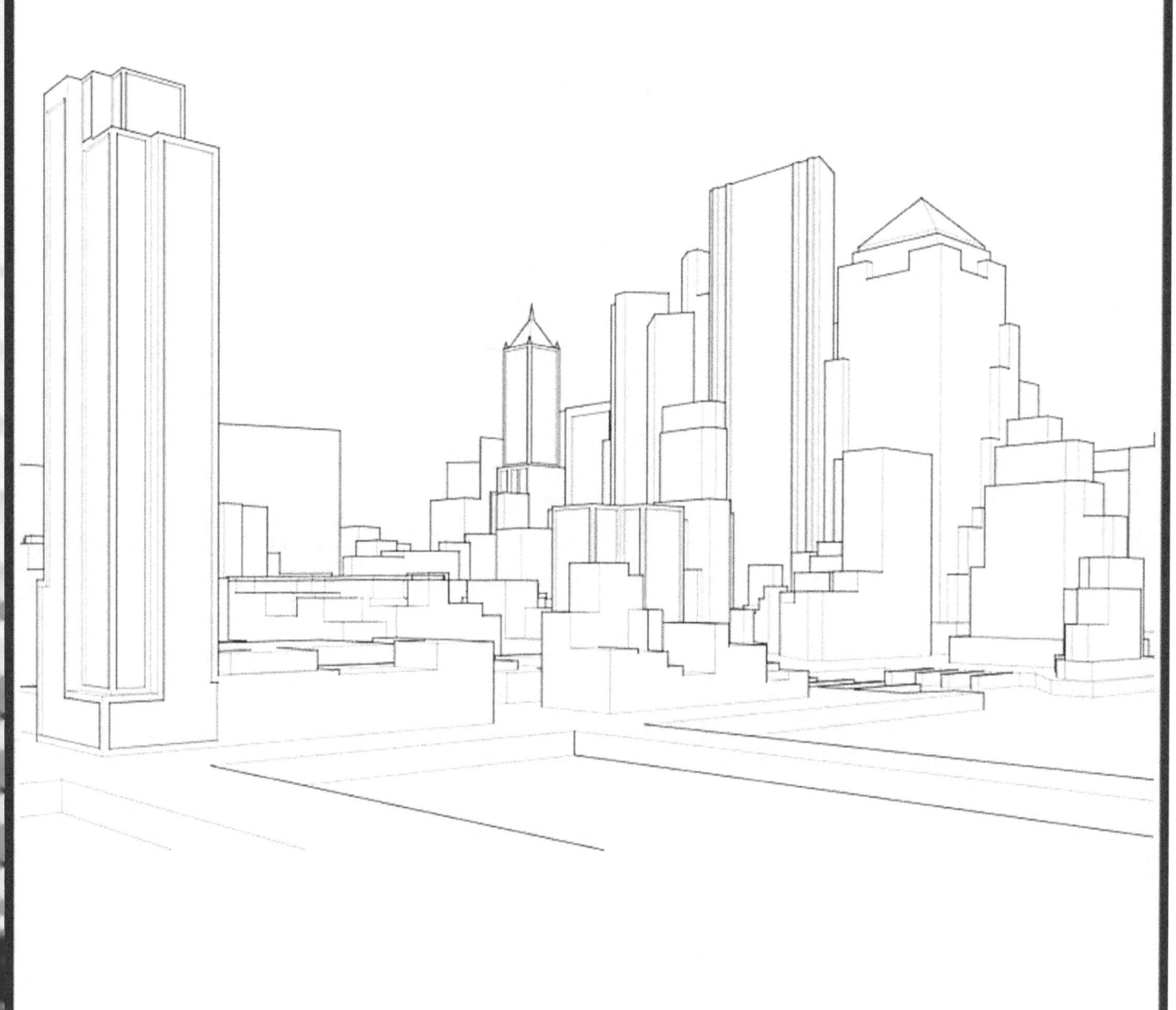

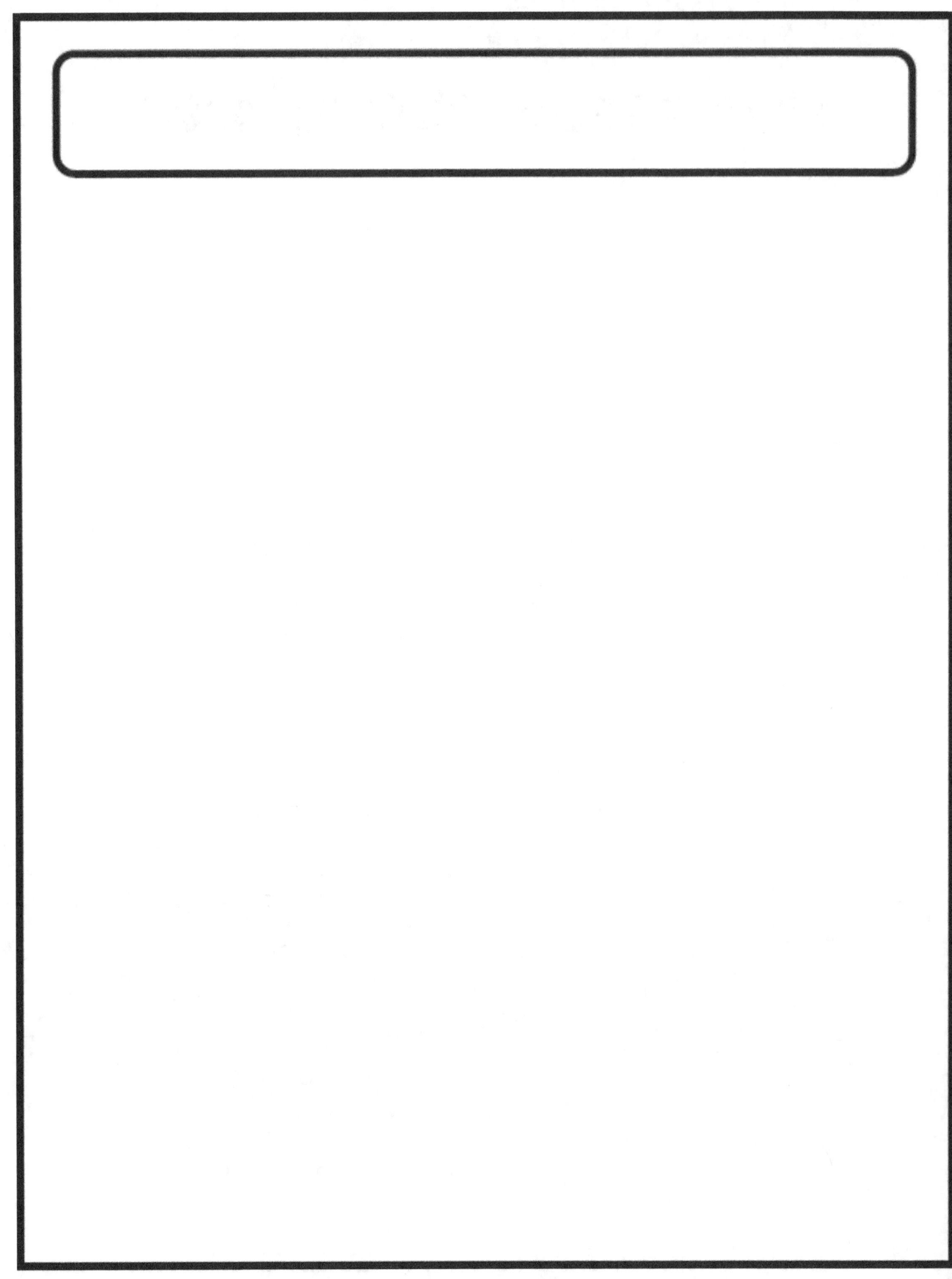

SKYSCRAPERS COLORING BOOK

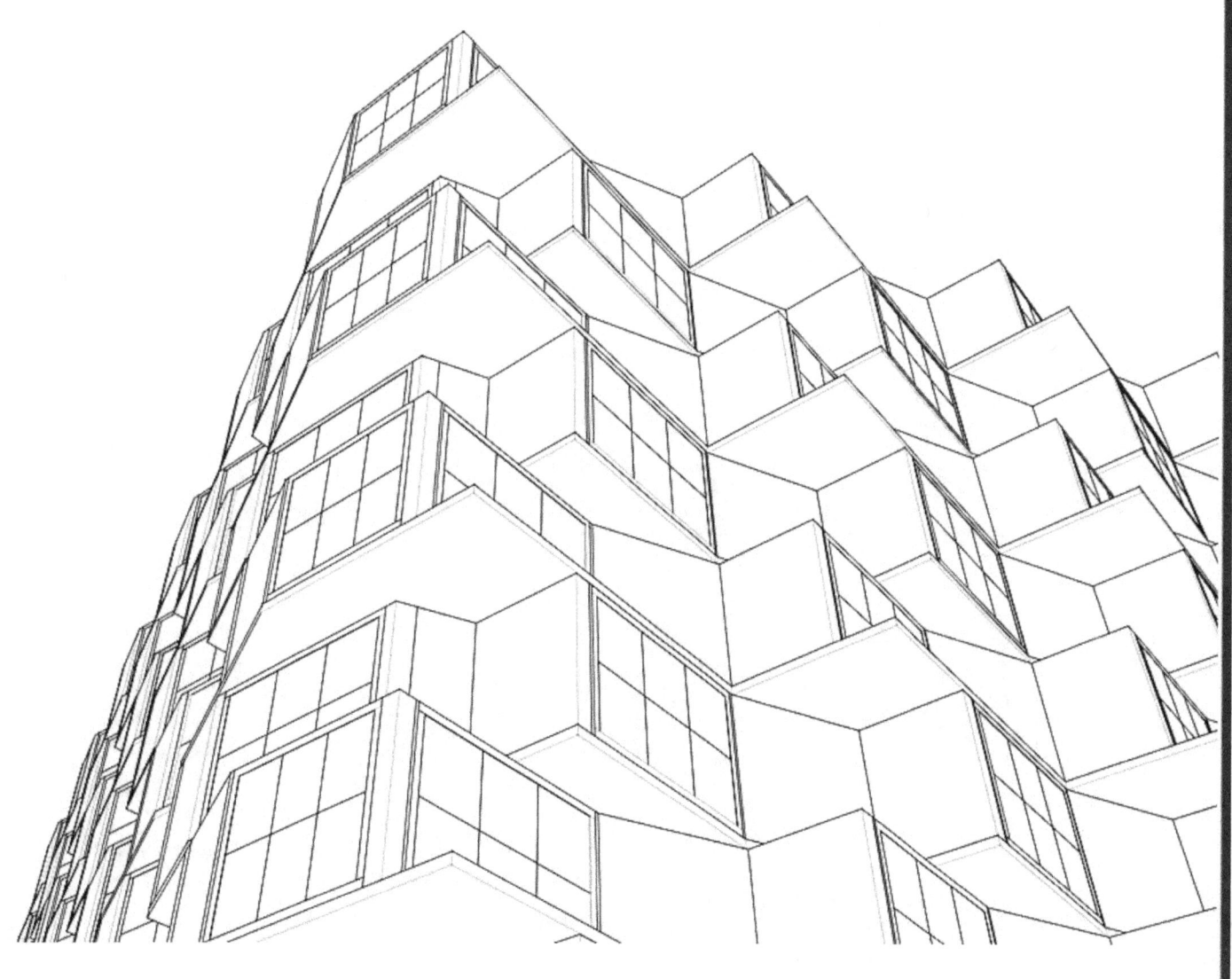

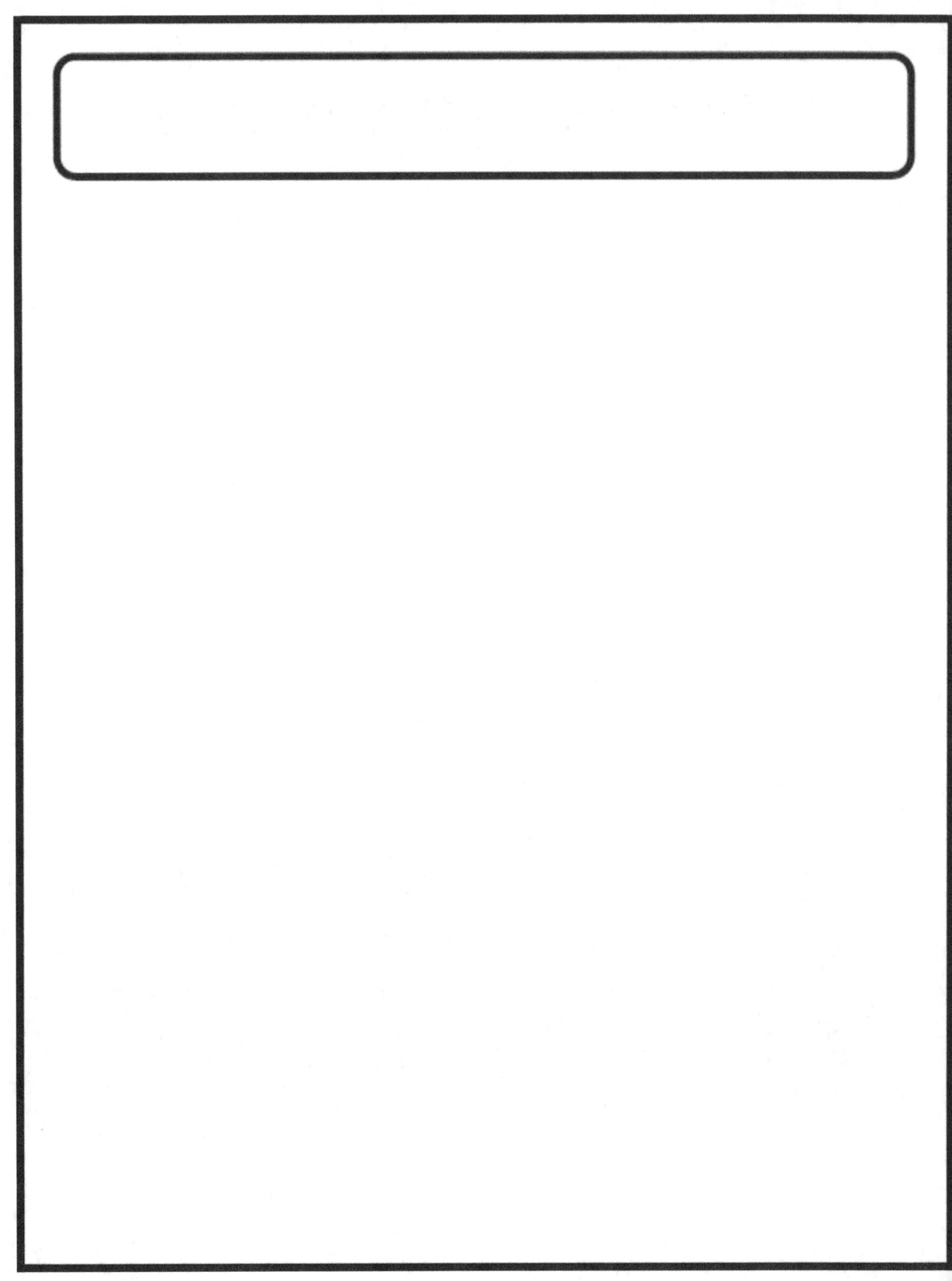

SKYSCRAPERS COLORING BOOK

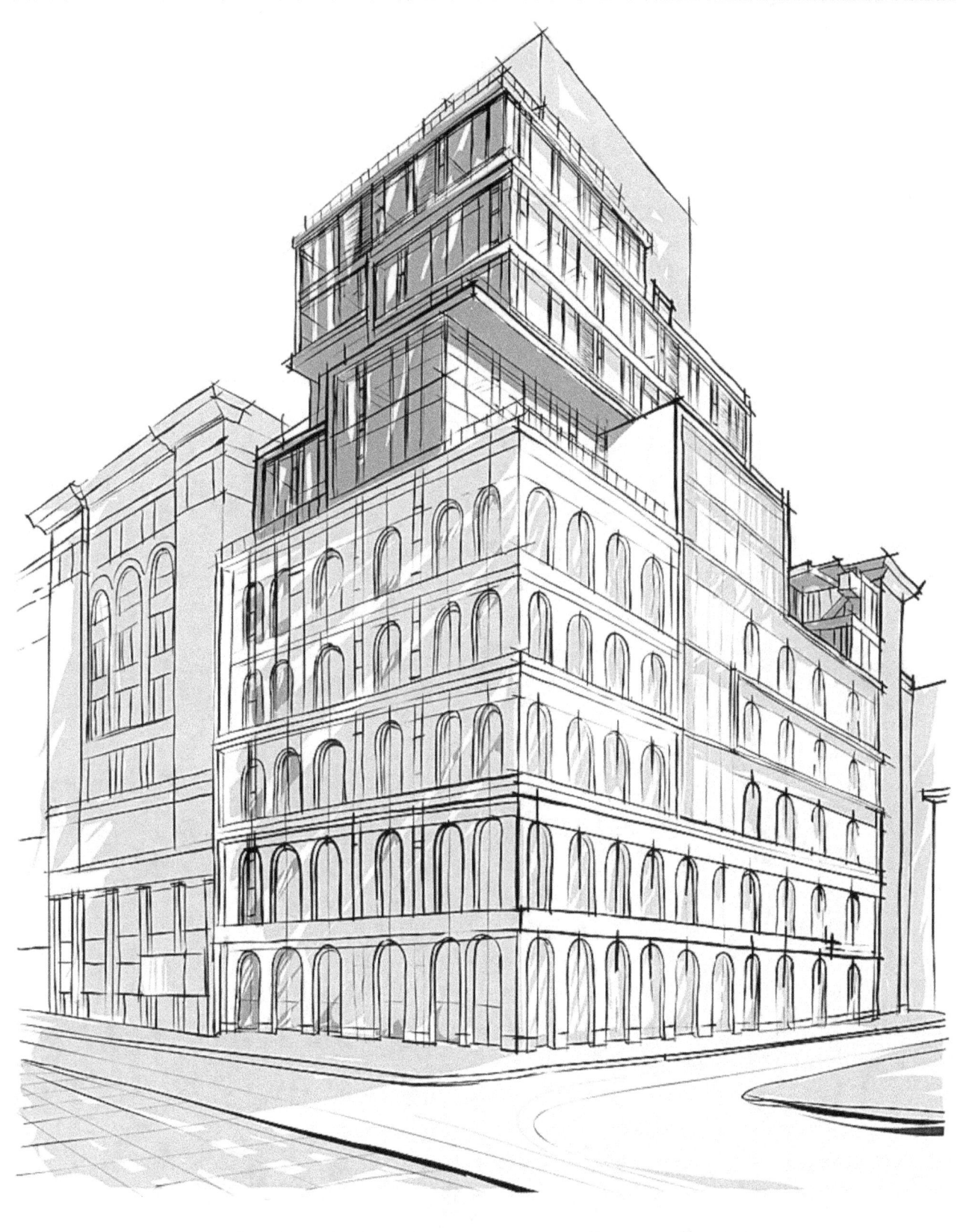

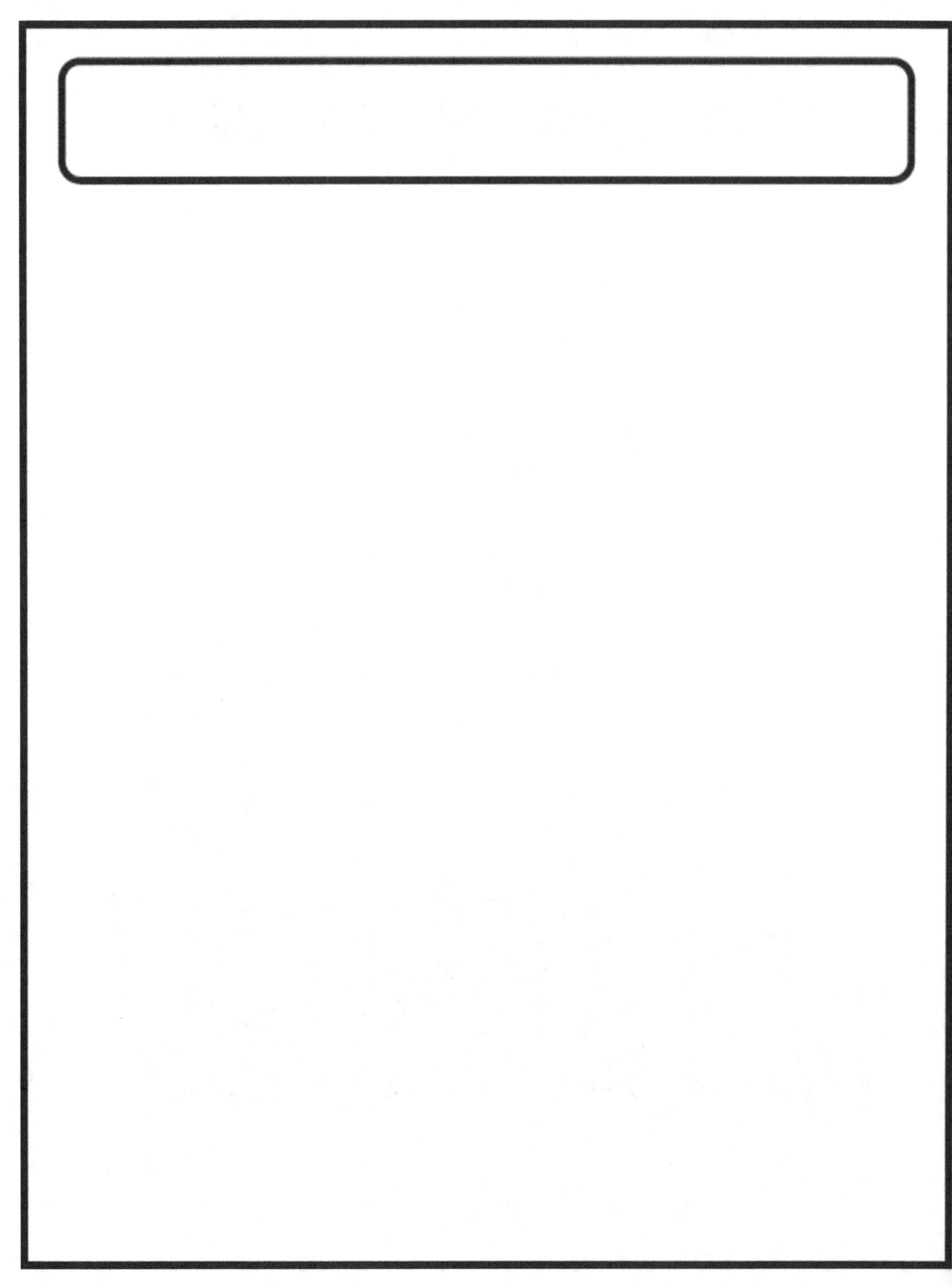

SKYSCRAPERS COLORING BOOK

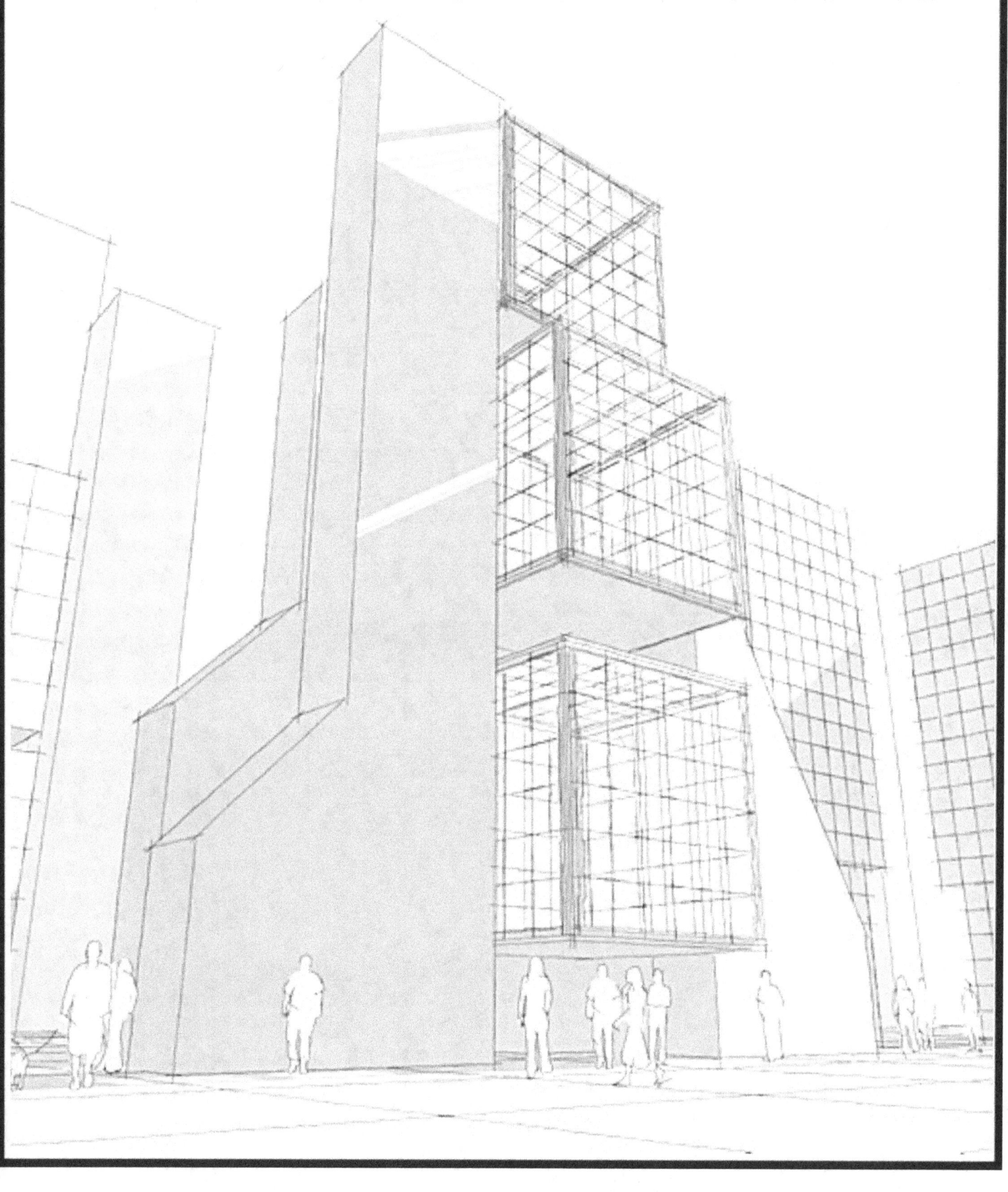

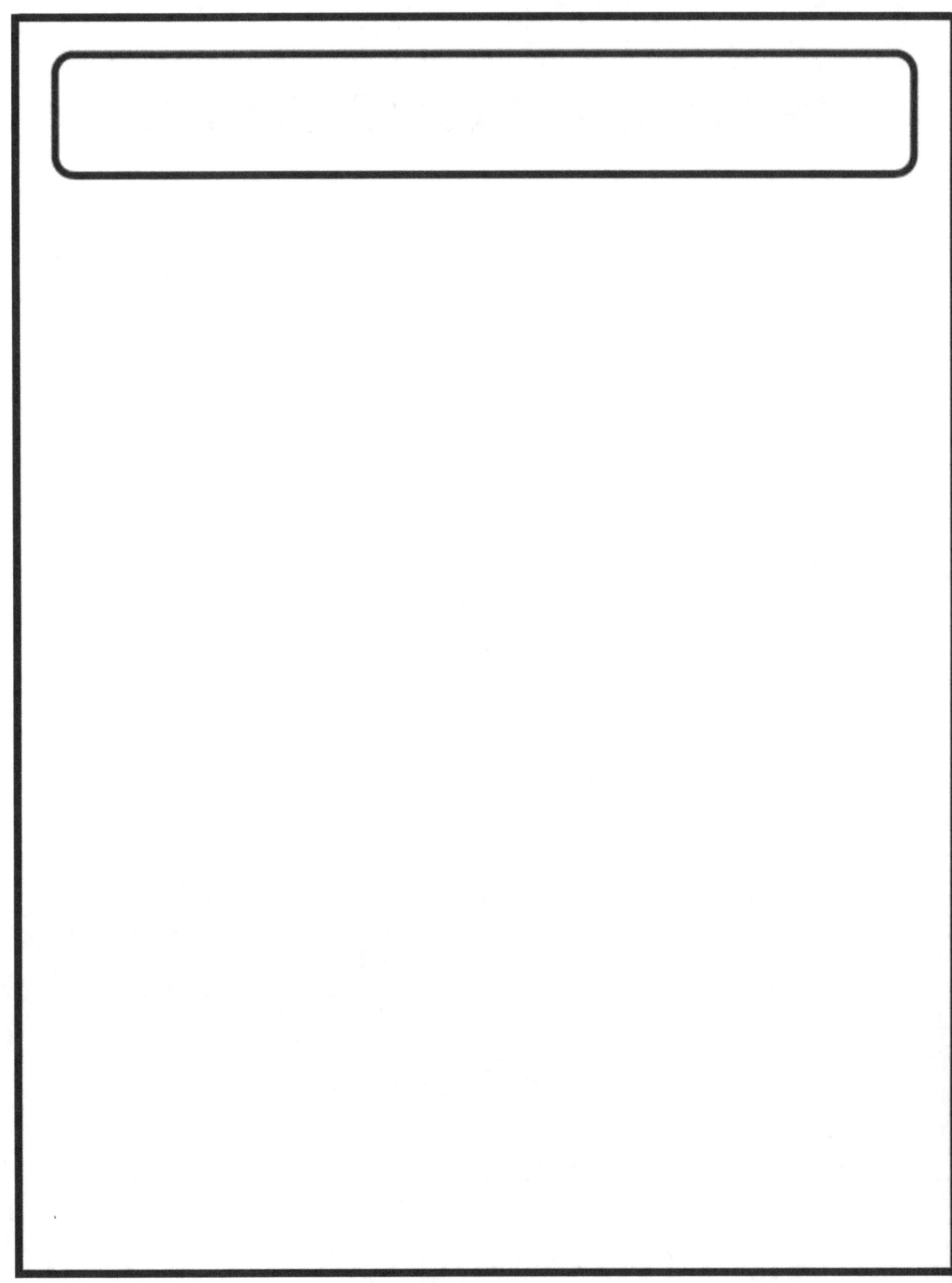

SKYSCRAPERS COLORING BOOK

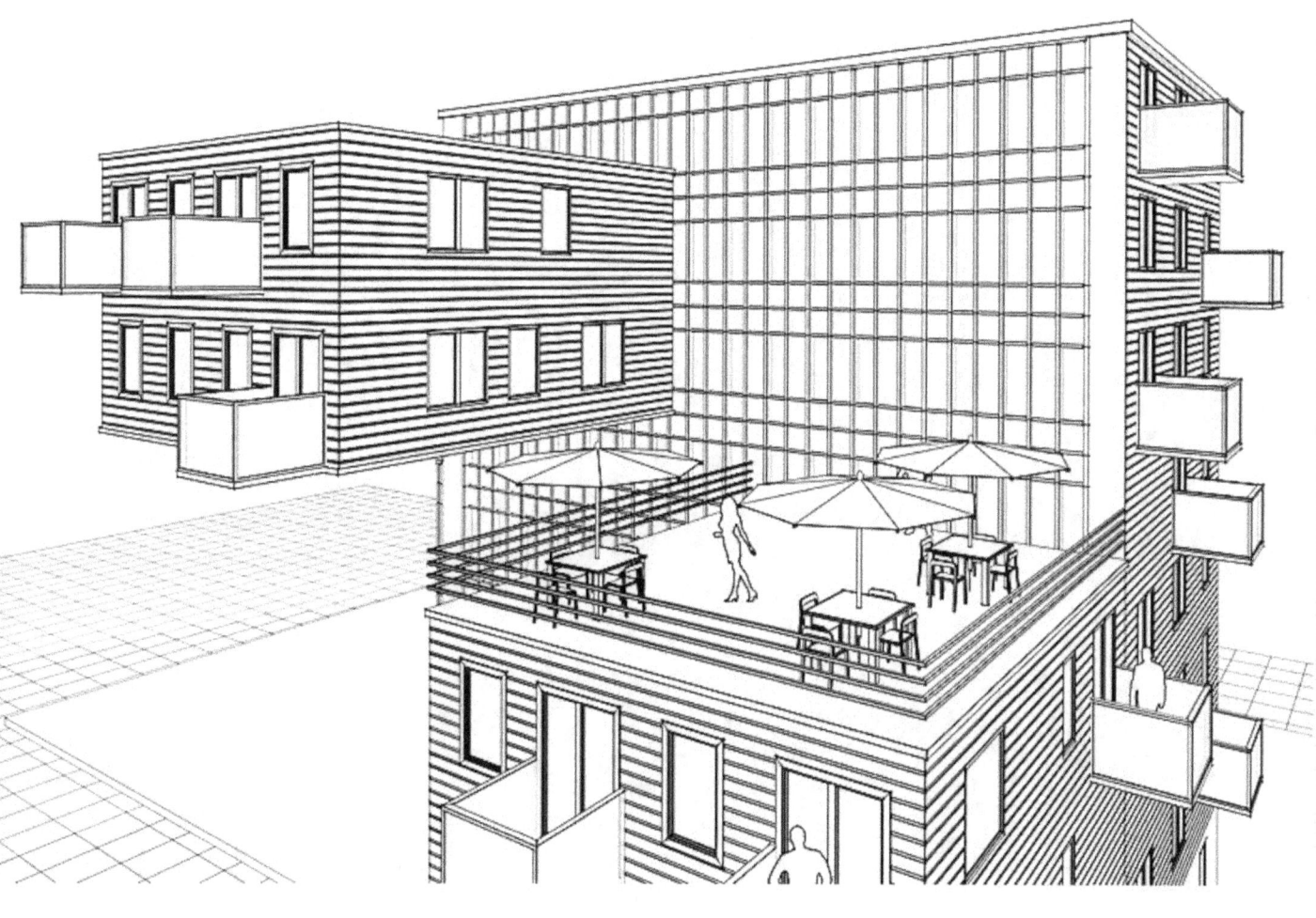

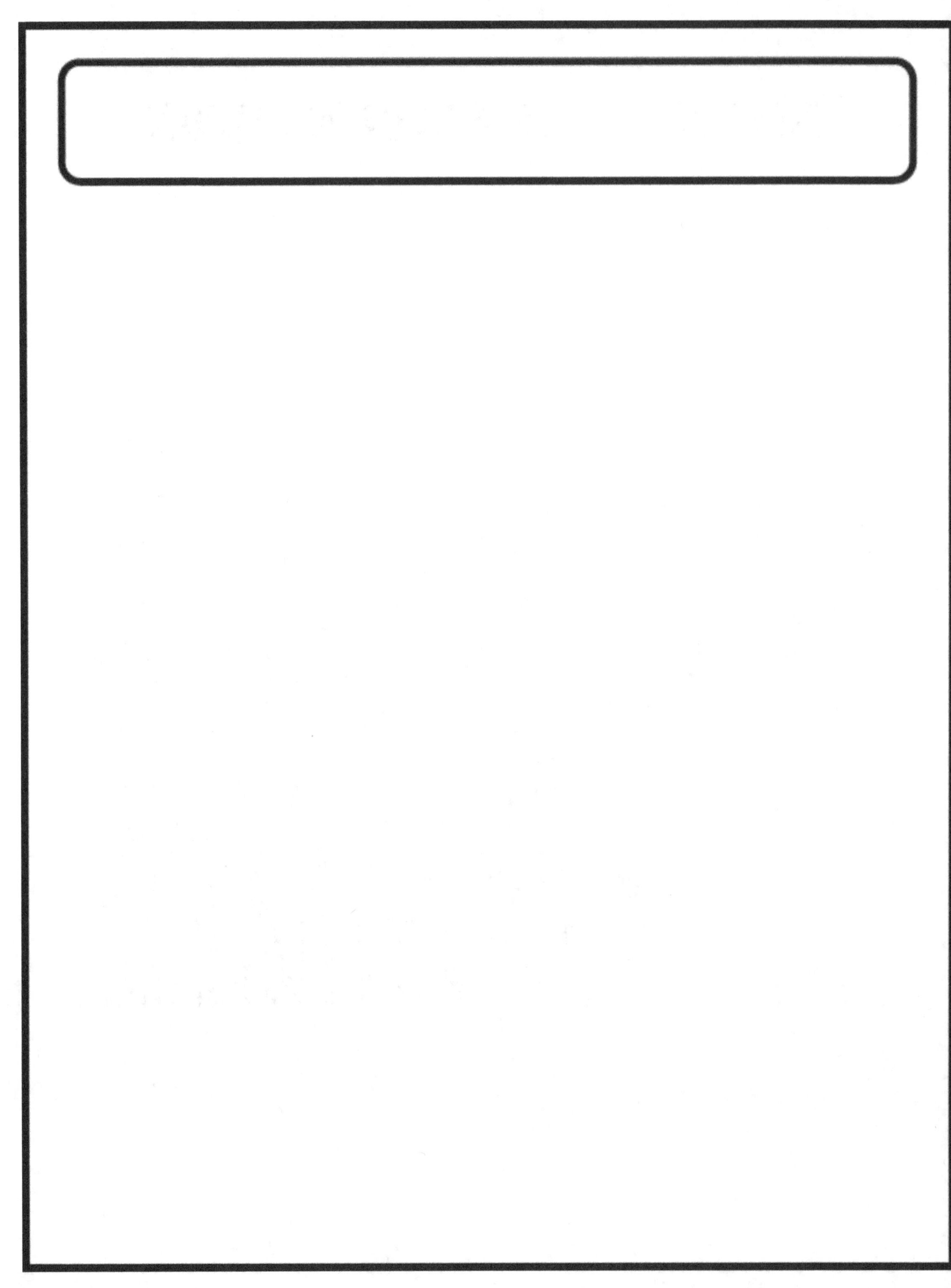

SKYSCRAPERS COLORING BOOK

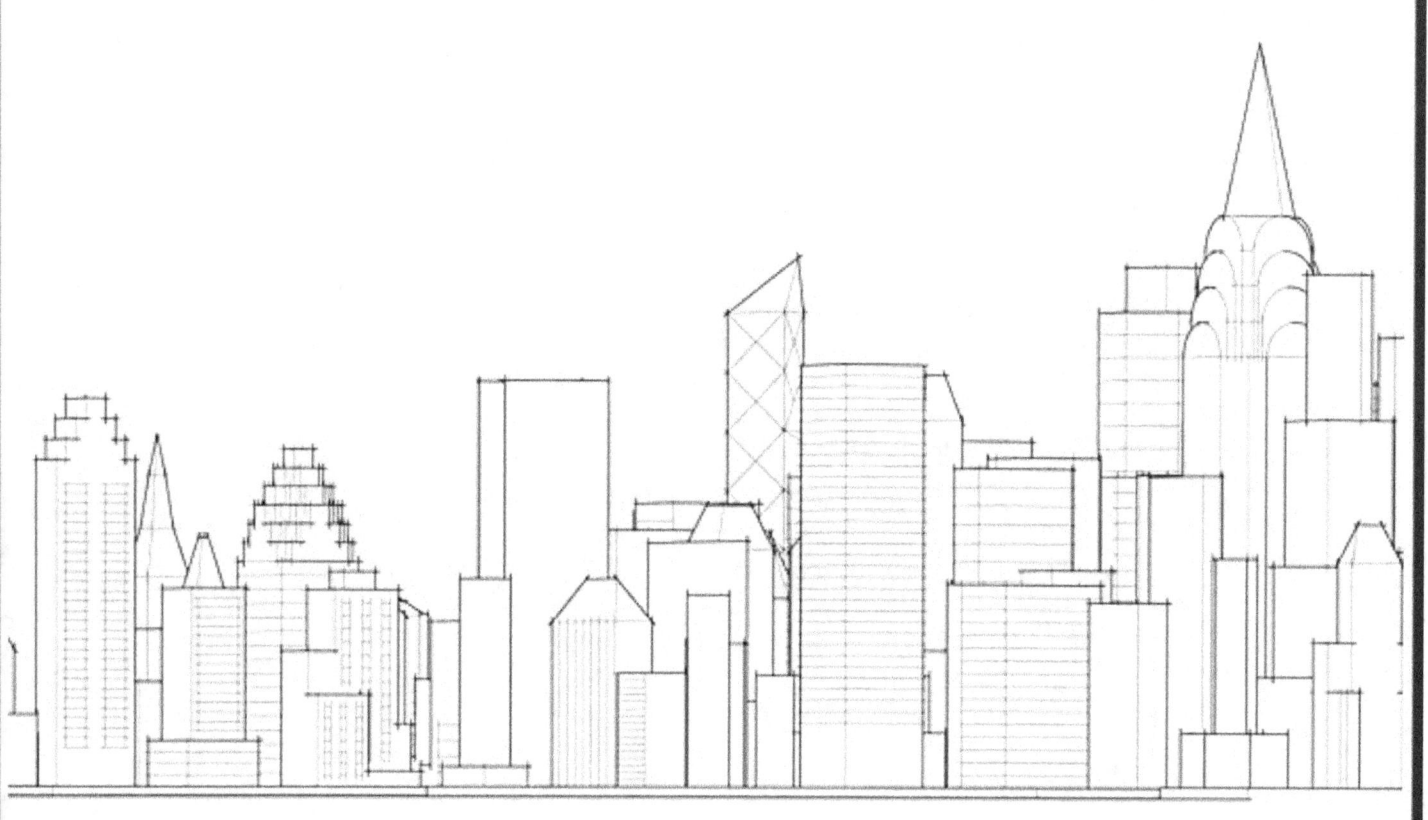

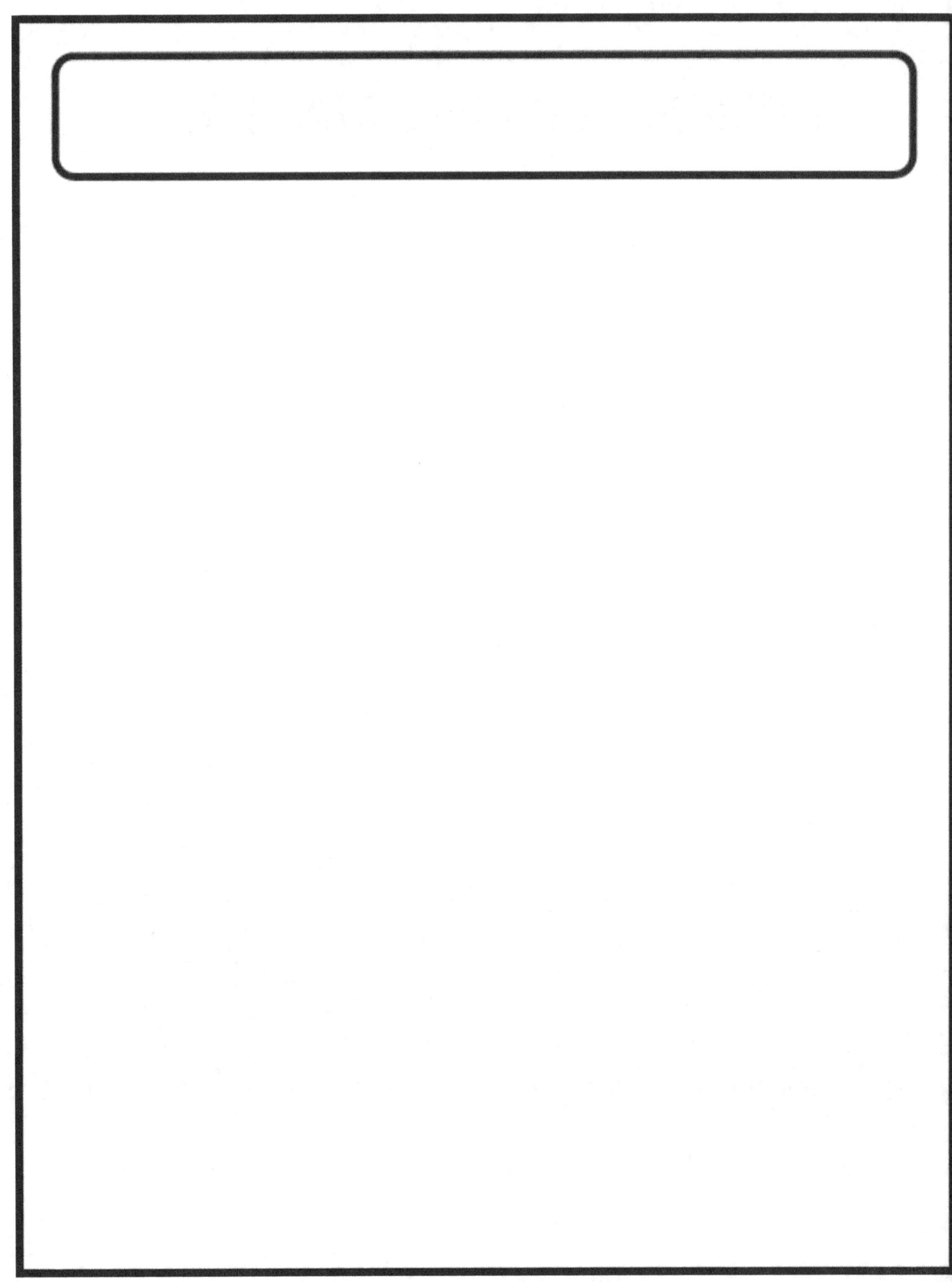

SKYSCRAPERS COLORING BOOK

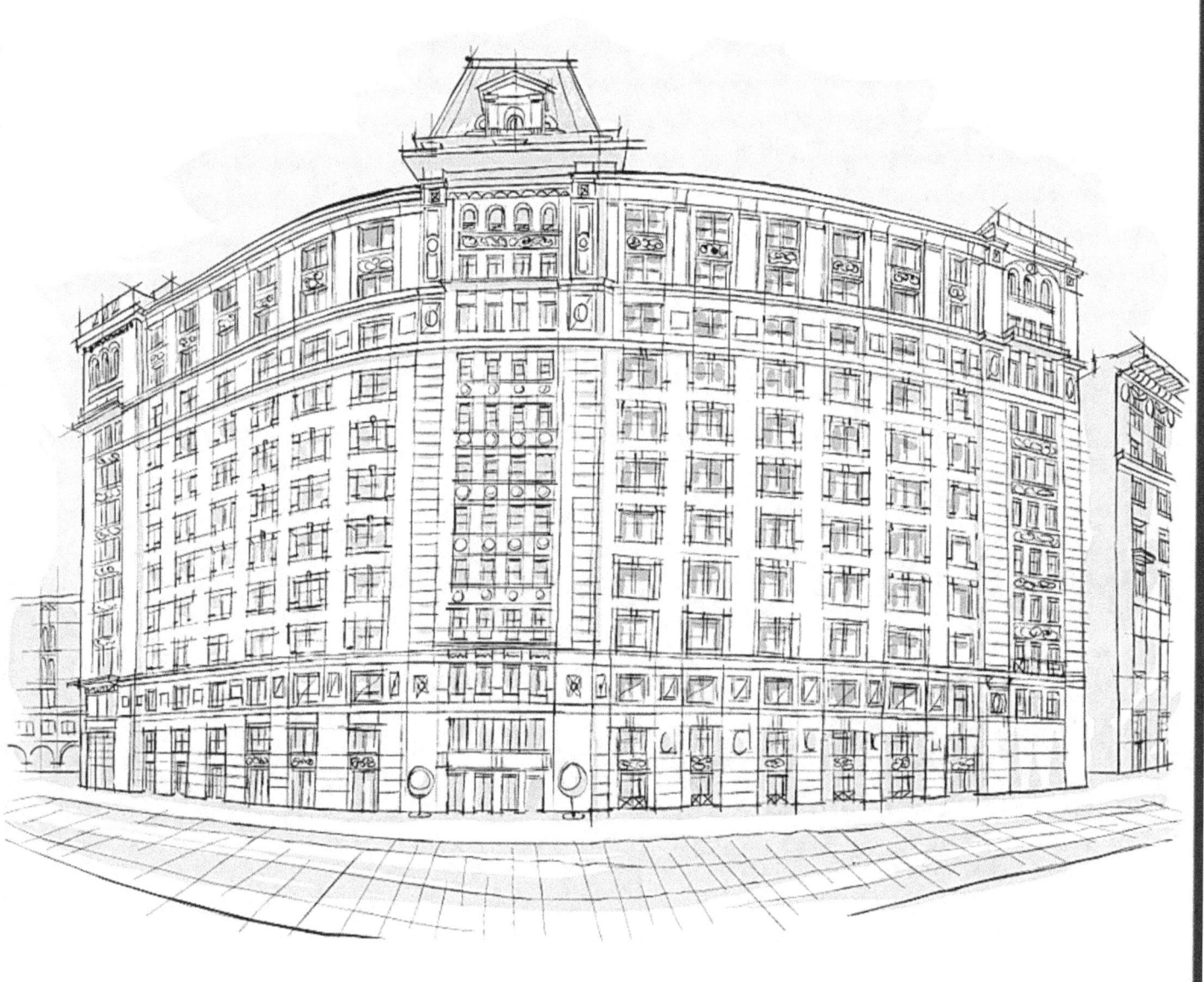

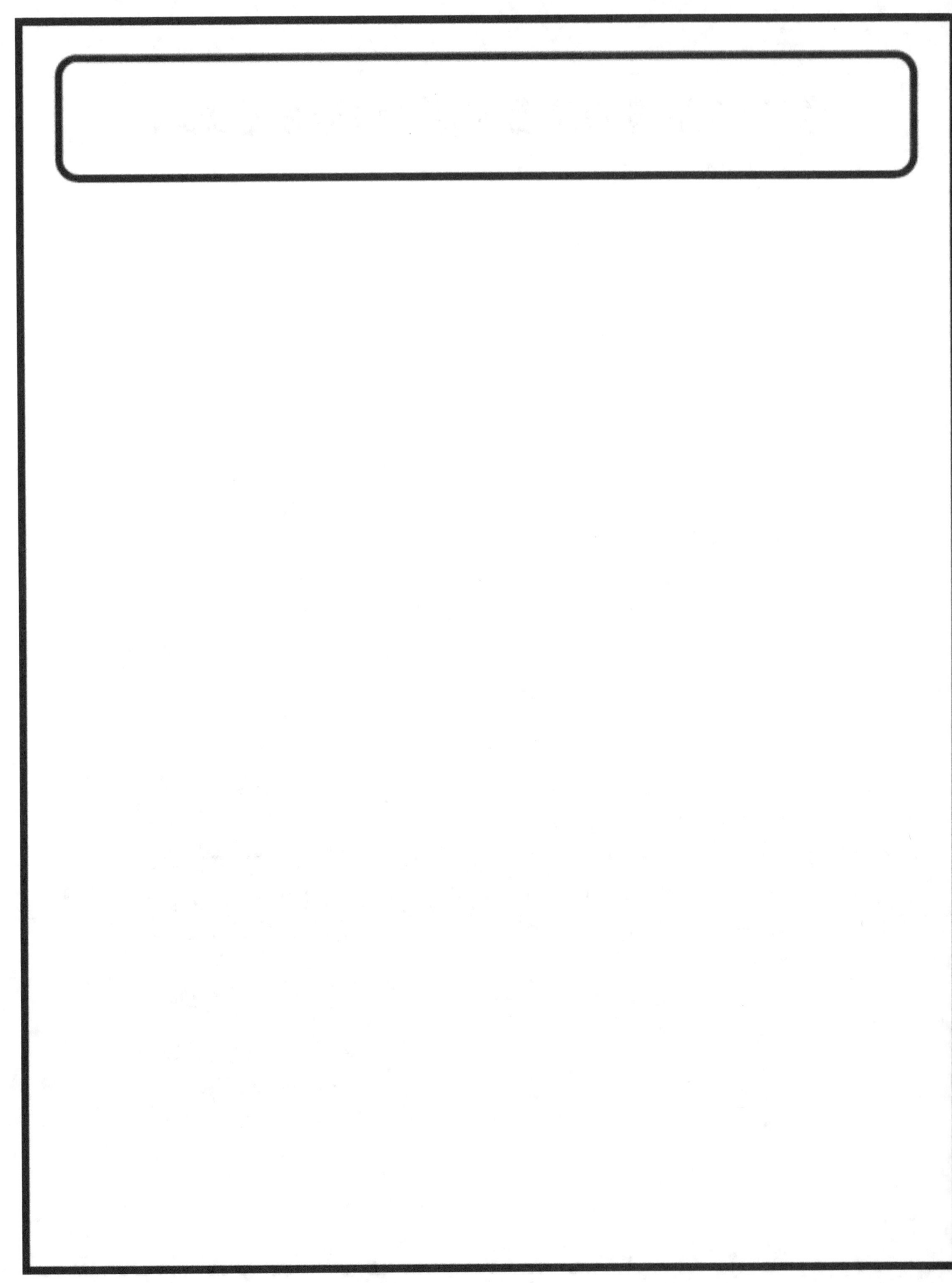

SKYSCRAPERS COLORING BOOK

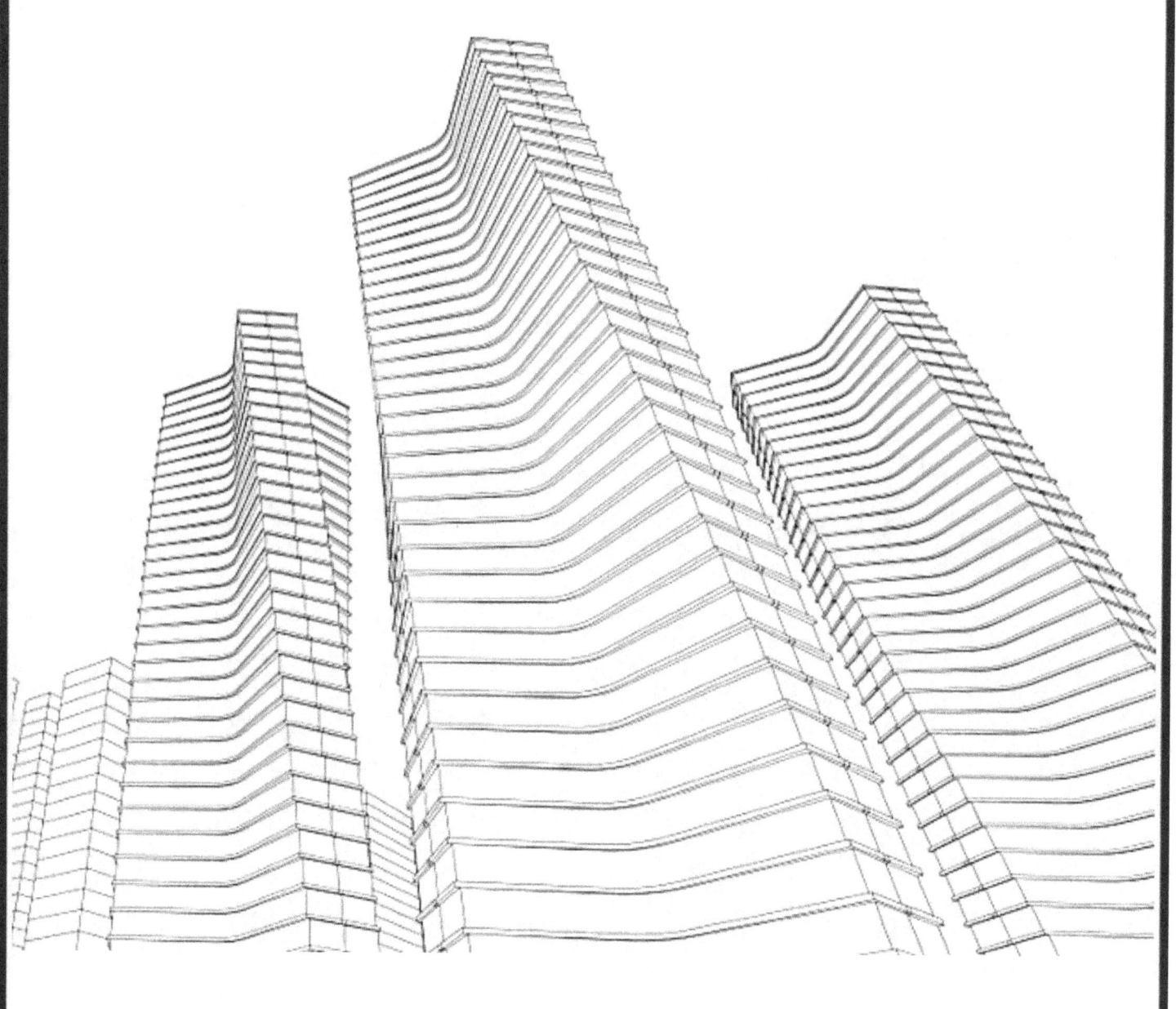

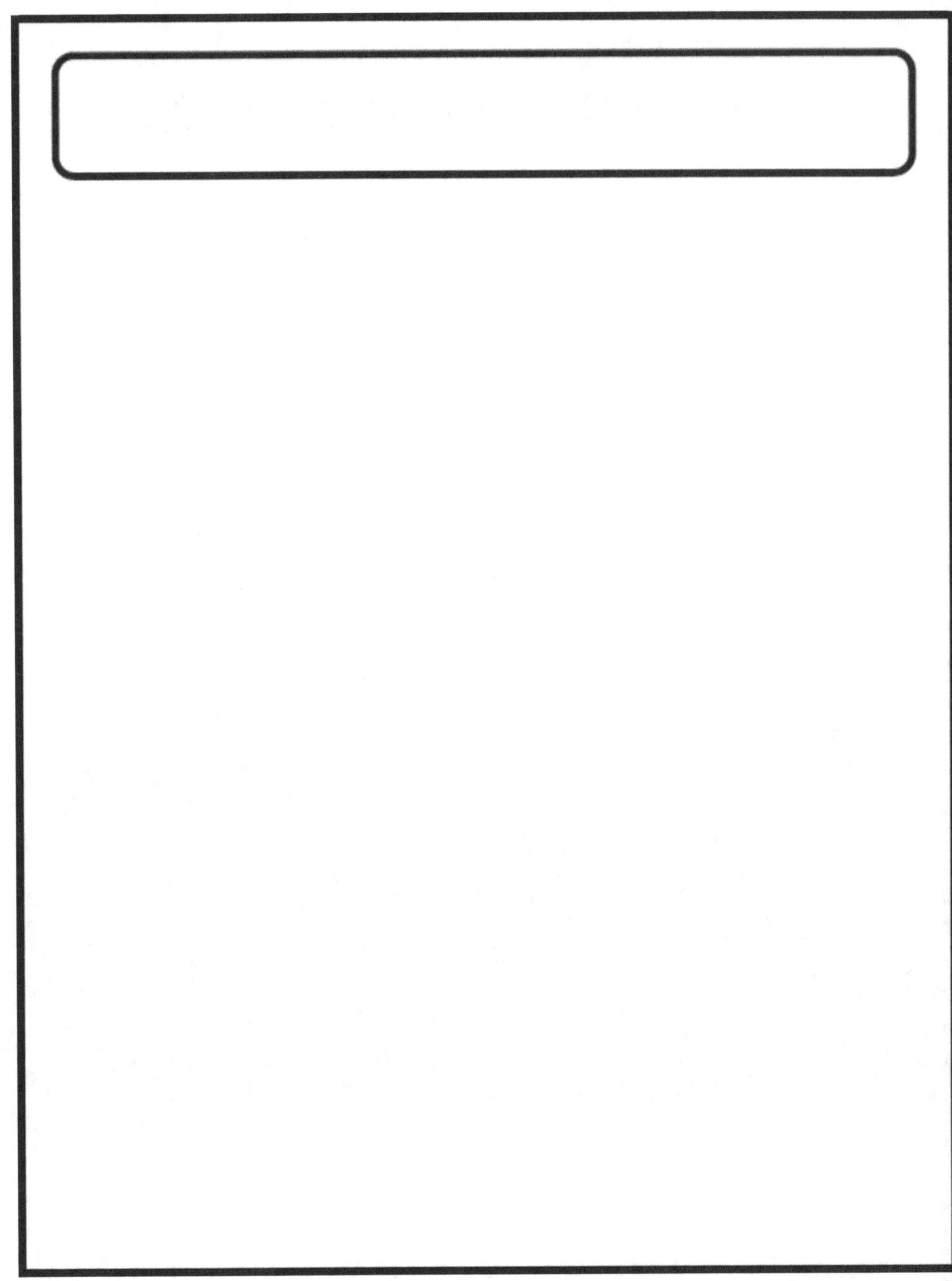

SKYSCRAPERS COLORING BOOK

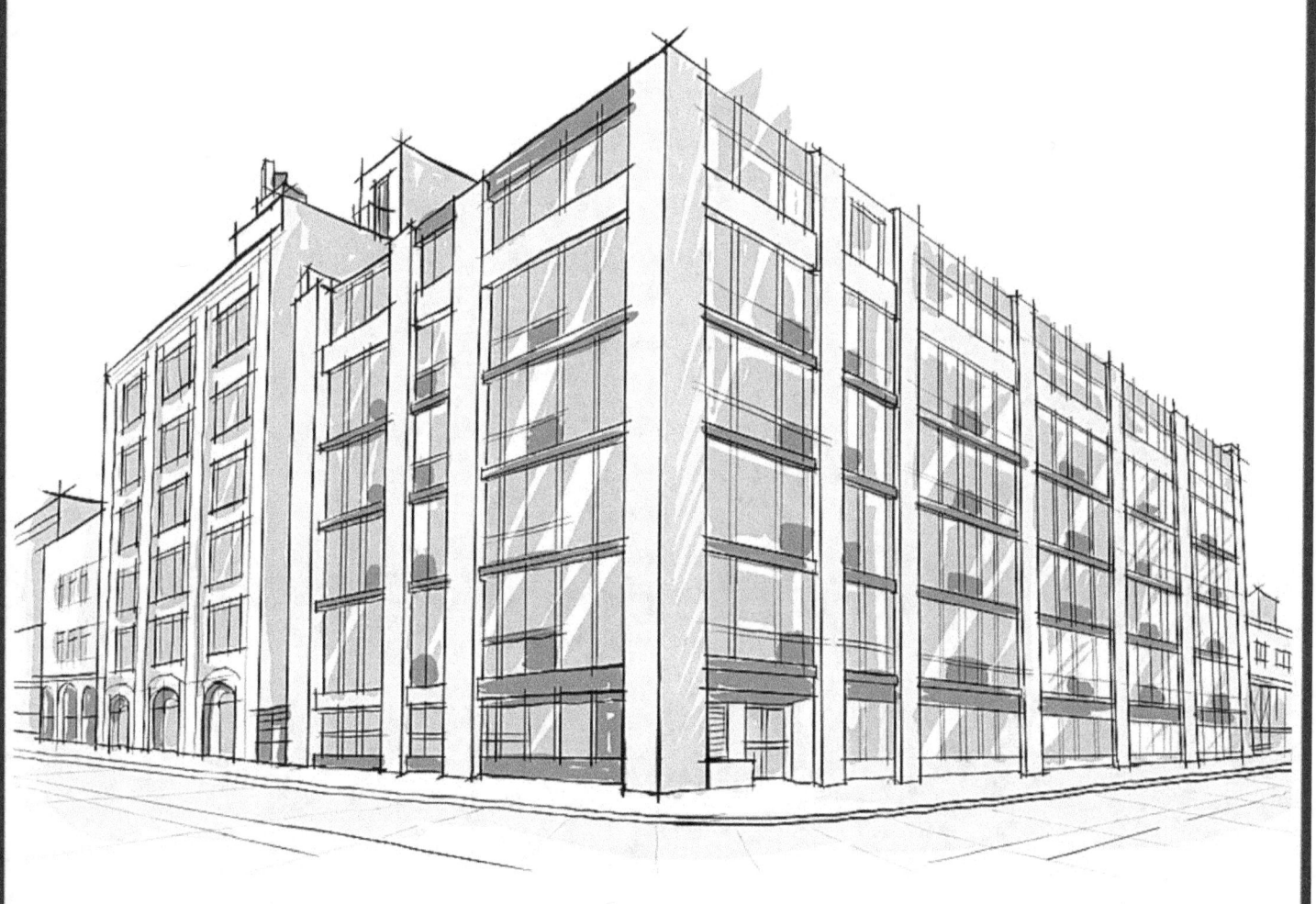

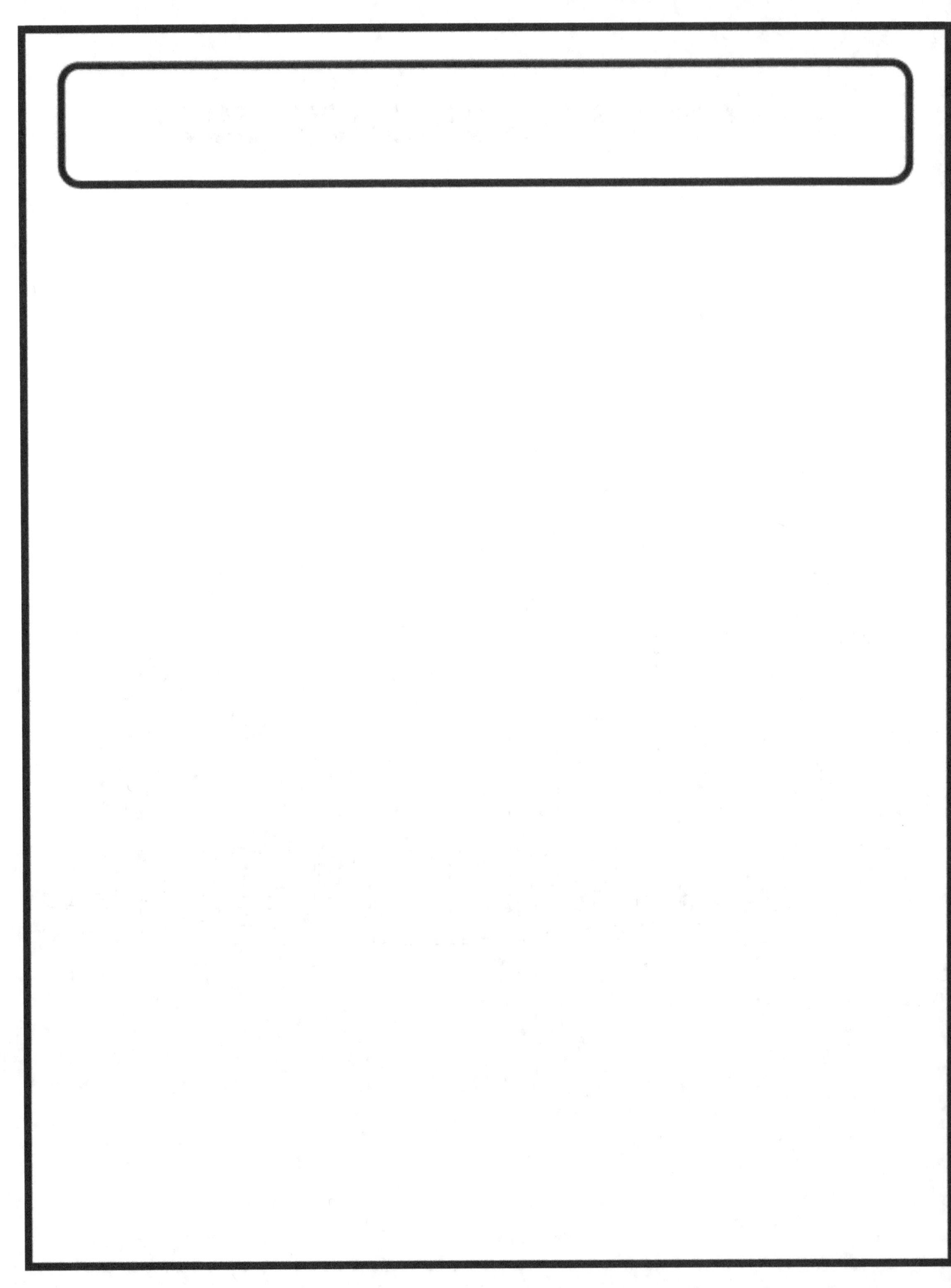

SKYSCRAPERS COLORING BOOK

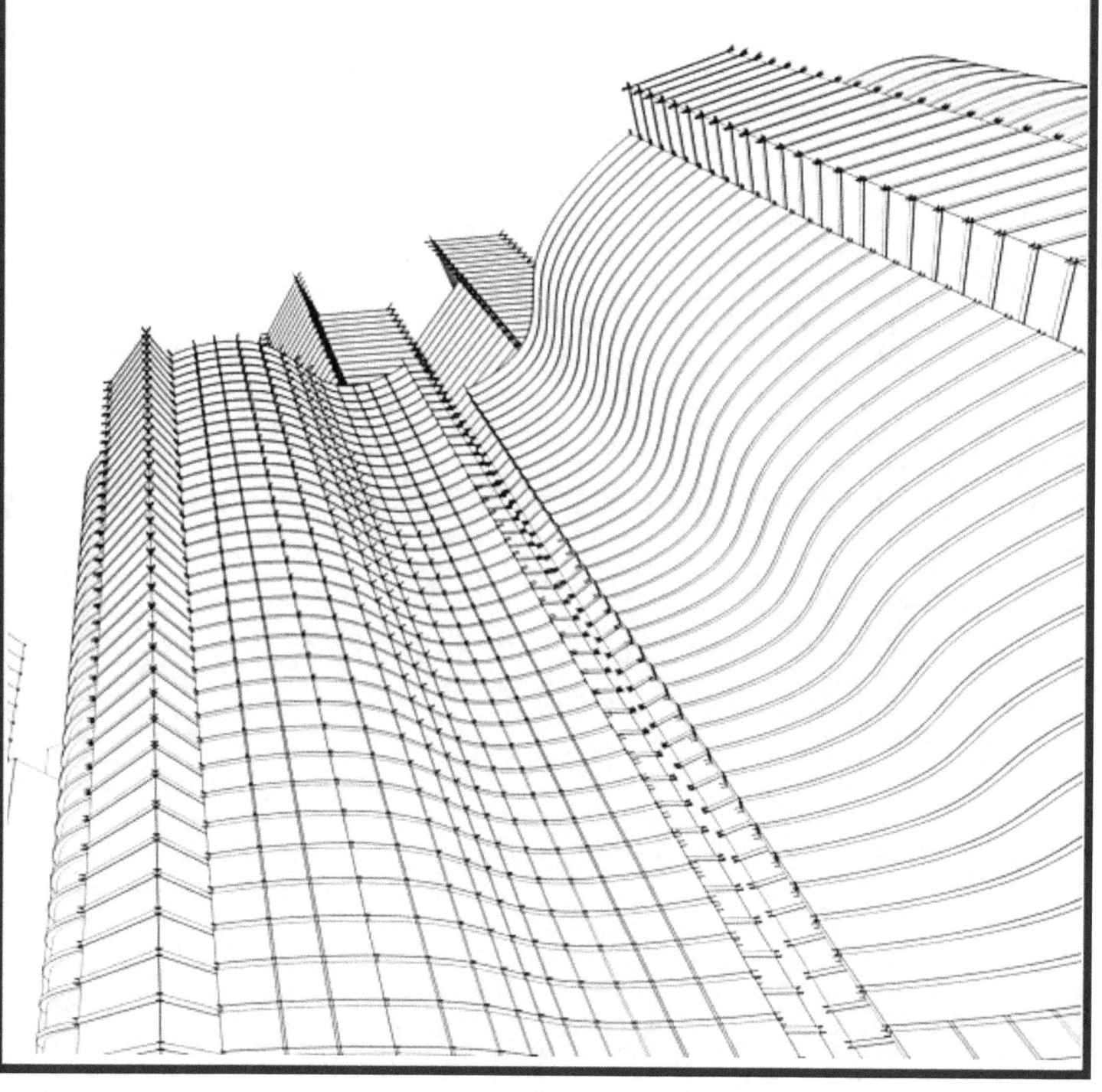

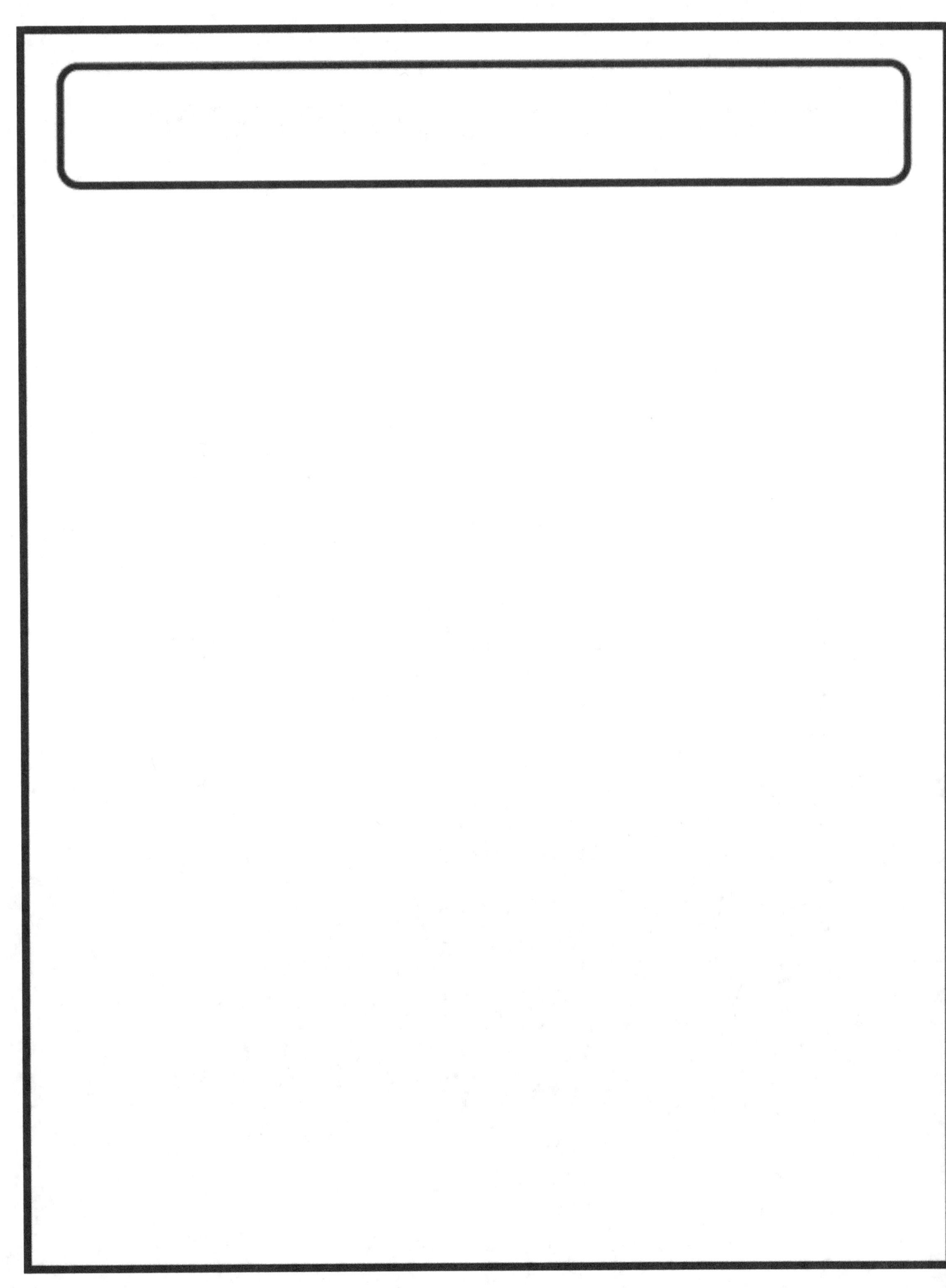

SKYSCRAPERS COLORING BOOK

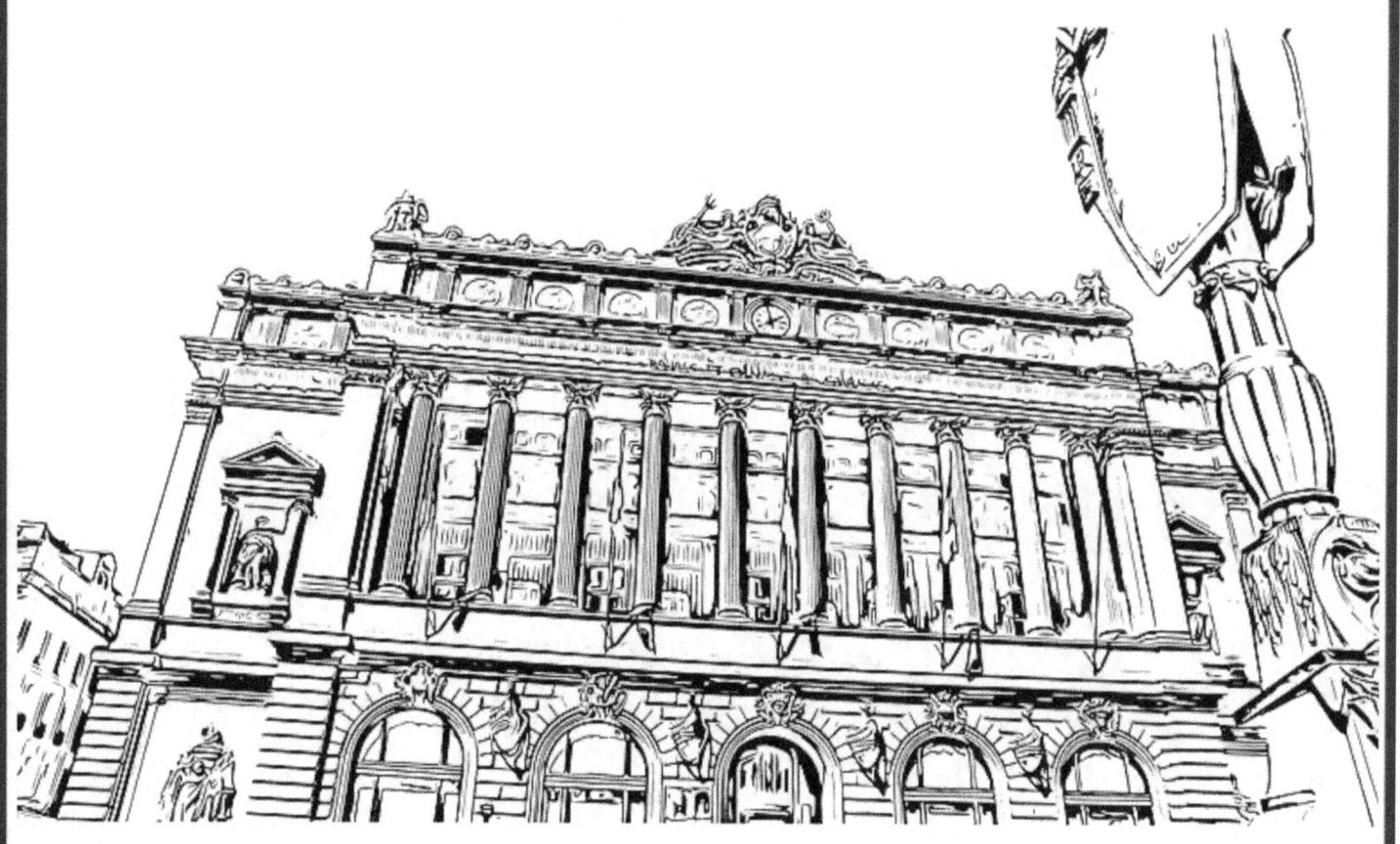

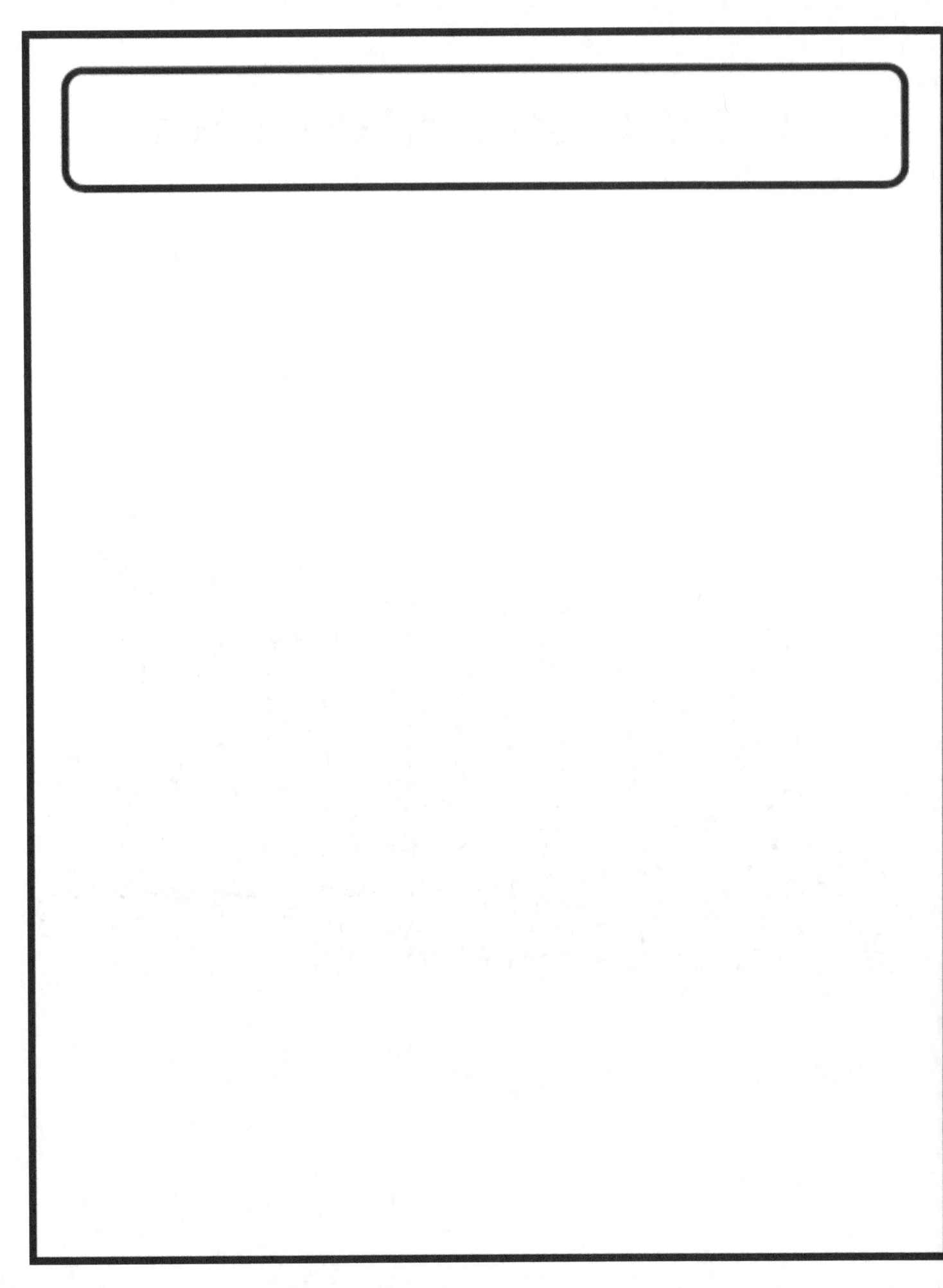

SKYSCRAPERS COLORING BOOK

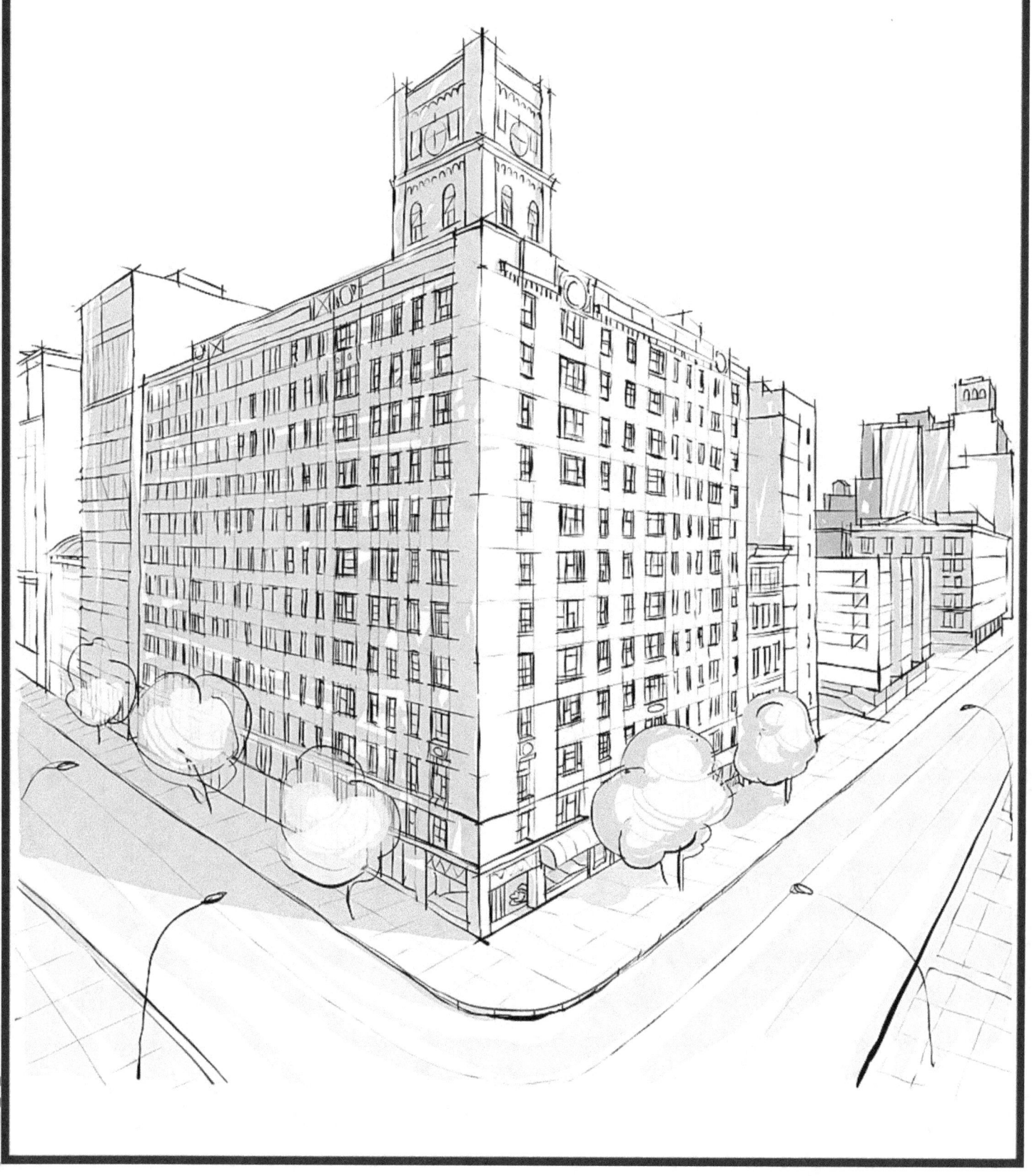

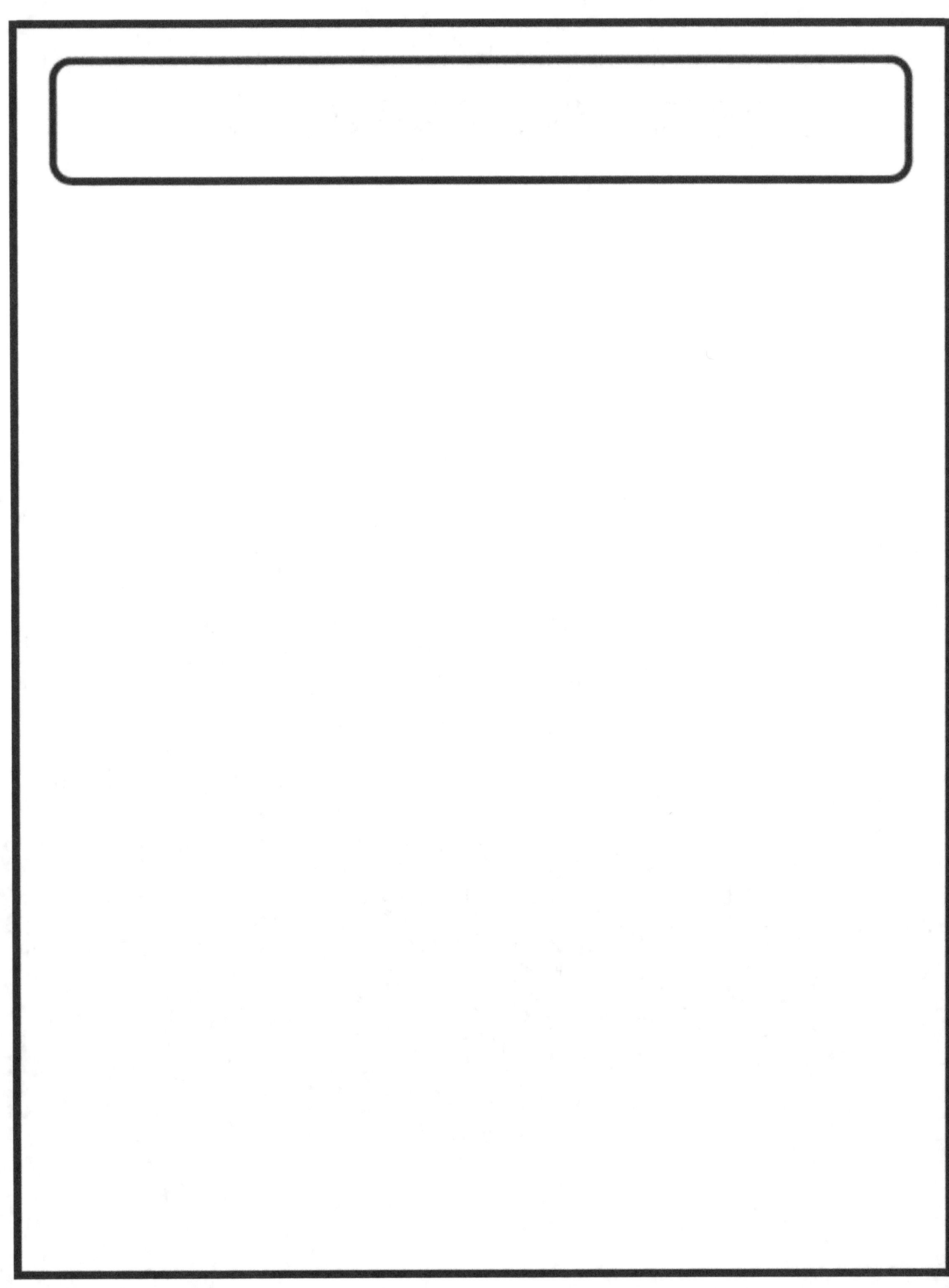

SKYSCRAPERS COLORING BOOK

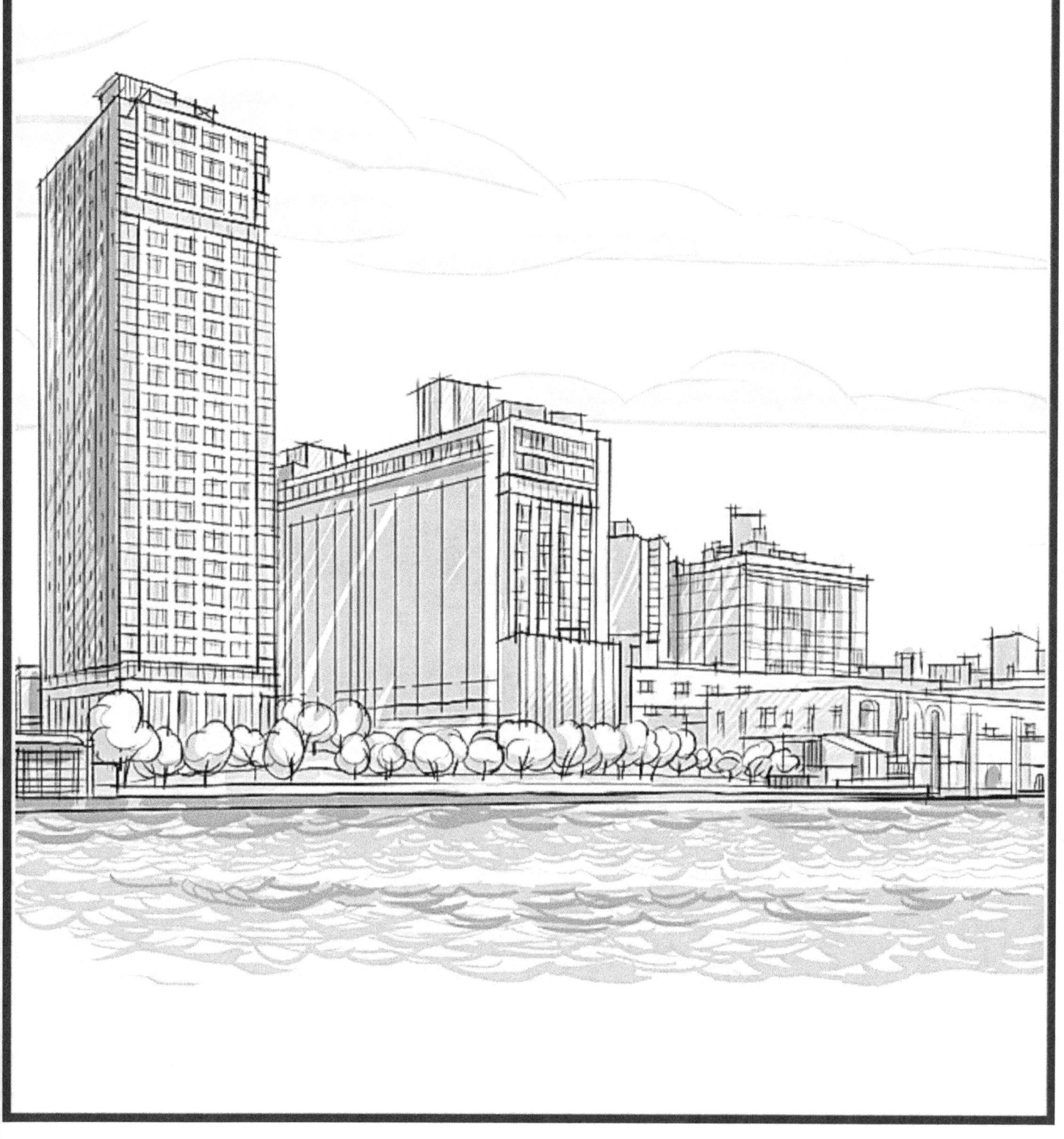

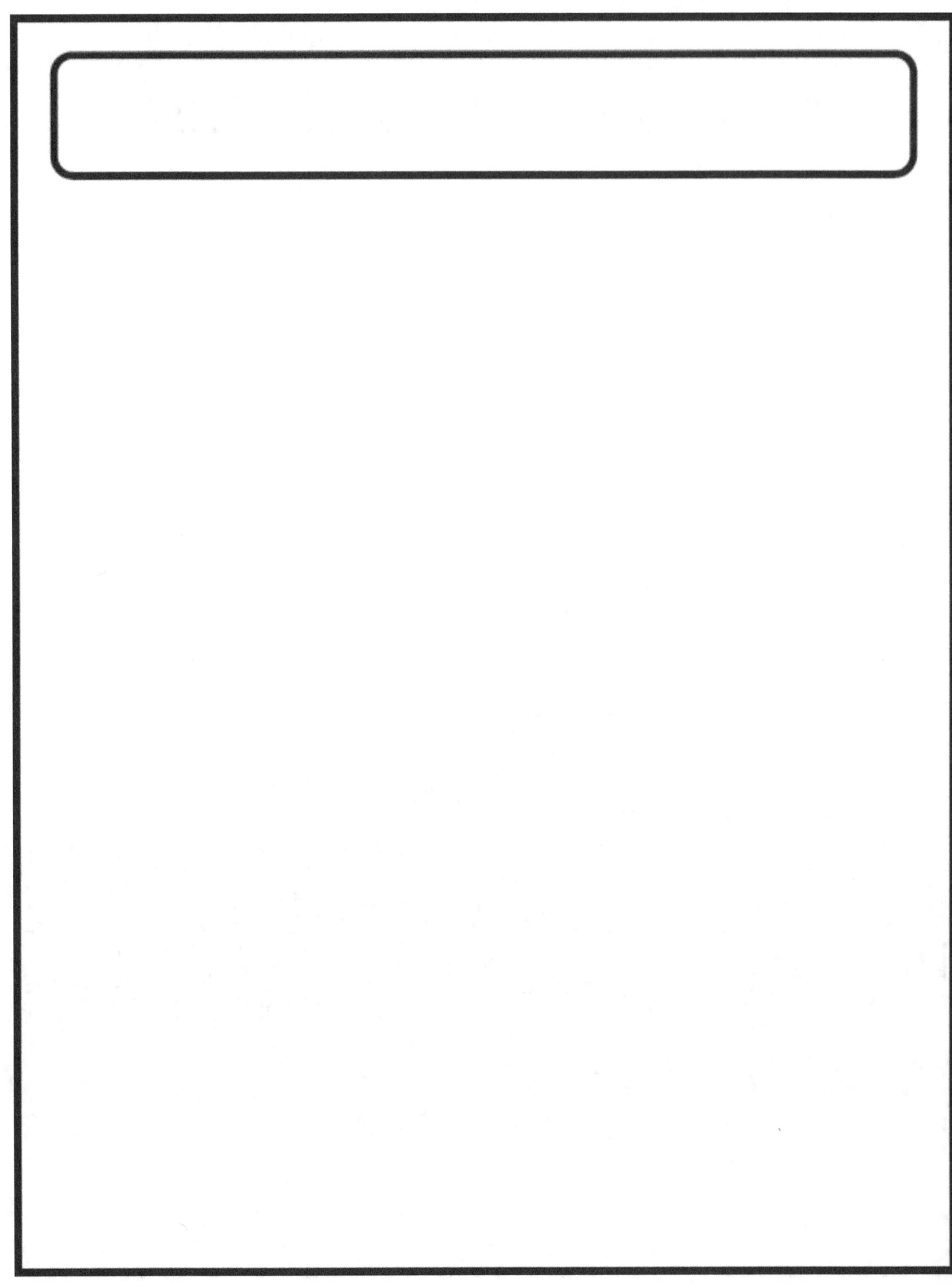

SKYSCRAPERS COLORING BOOK

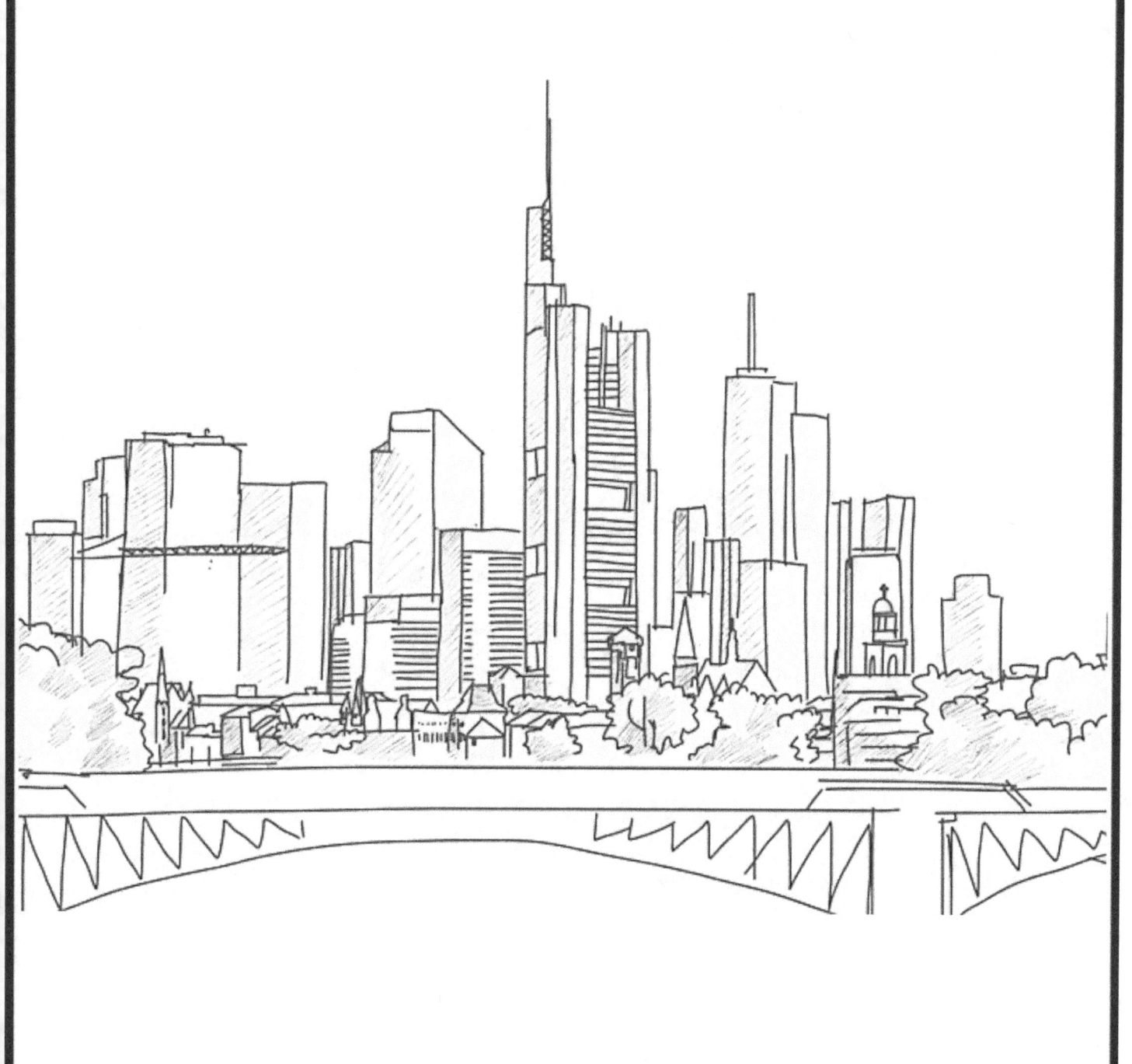

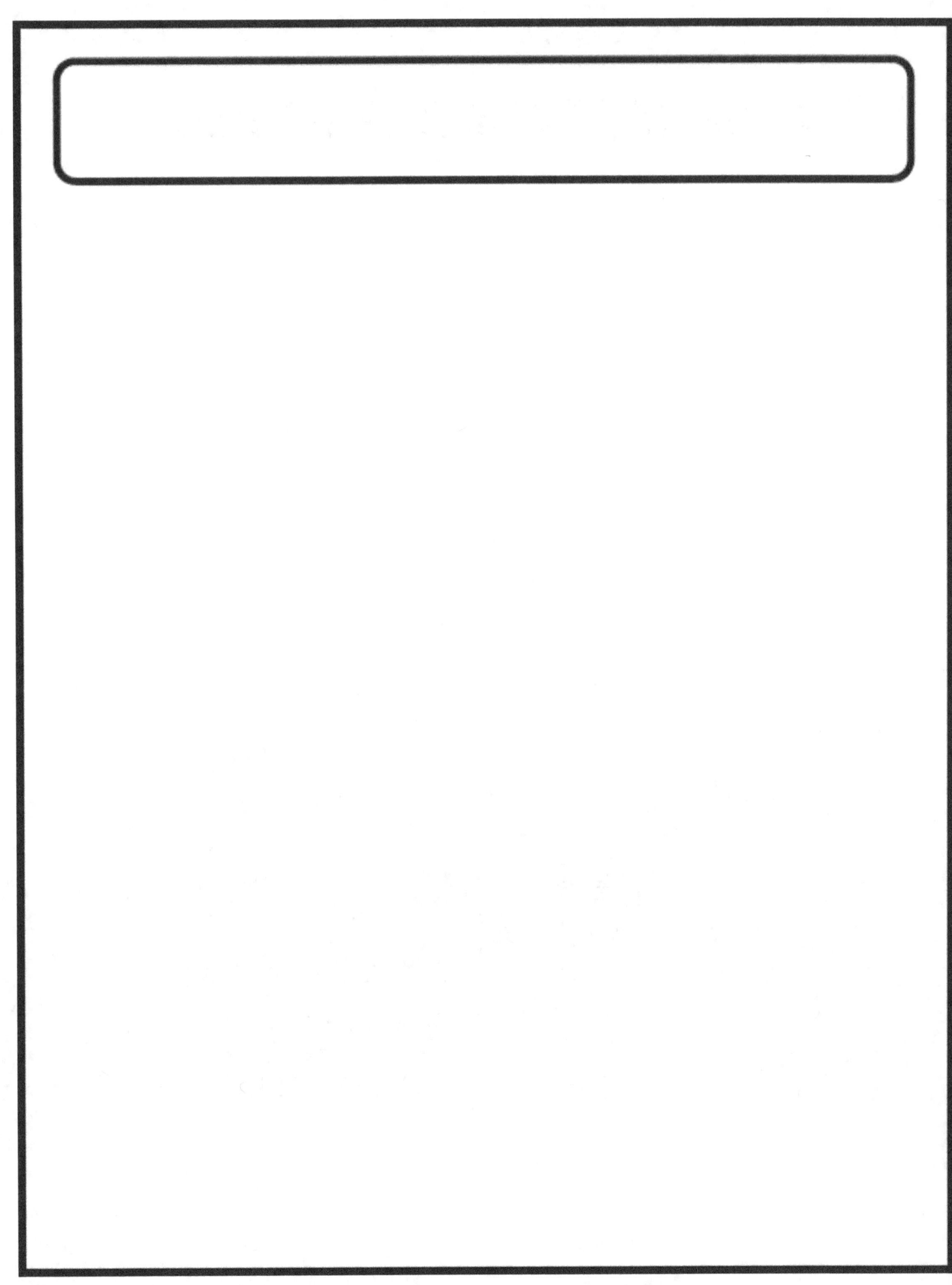

Enjoying this Notebook?

Please leave *Black Rose Press House* a review because we would love to know your thought, feedback, and opinions to create better products for you.
Please share how you creatively use your notebooks and journals.

THANKS
FOR YOUR SUPPORT

Scan This Qr Code And Visit Our Author Page At-
amazon.com